D0888268

Book of Exploration

Using the Inner Outings Method
and Diarist's Deck of 33 Cards

Charlene Geiss
Claudia Jessup

NEW WORLD LIBRARY
NOVATO, CALIFORNIA

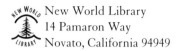 New World Library
14 Pamaron Way
Novato, California 94949

Design by Mary Ann Casler
Front cover art by Charlene Geiss

Library of Congress Cataloging-in-Publication Data available.

First printing, September 2002
Package ISBN 1-57731-220-1
Printed in Hong Kong
Distributed to the trade by Publishers Group West

10 9 8 7 6 5 4 3 2 1

Contents

Additional Resources for the Diarist

Prologue

*D*ear Diarist,

   Are you ready to embark on a journey? I'm inviting you on expeditions —"inner outings"— into your own interior landscape where your emotions, desires, thoughts, fears, and motivations live and thrive. The Inner Outings experience is going to be heady, and full of heart, and completely different for each and every person reading this book.

   Trips to uncharted inner realms are merely an aspect of the exciting activity that lies ahead. You'll learn to use your journal as a place for self-exploration that, in turn, will lead to transformation. Your diary will become a special, safe harbor that you can sail into anytime, anywhere, for the rest of your life. The Diarist's Deck and *Book of Exploration* will make it all possible.

   Let me first tell you a bit about the Diarists' Workshop, which was born in 1997. I'd been keeping a diary and studying every facet of journal writing, but for more than thirty years I was a secret diarist. No one saw my journals; I kept them locked in a cabinet. Then one night, at a large dinner party at my house, the conversation turned to journal writing and my husband Bruce urged me to show him — for the first time — and the others my journals. With trepidation I brought them out and passed around dozens of my personal diaries. Every single person, I can honestly say, was fascinated by my unique approach, which incorporates writing with collage, photos, rubber stamps, and such. Nearly everyone at the table, both men and women, said they'd take a class if I'd offer one.

Soon after, I started teaching an evening class that evolved into a series of classes, both private and at the local community college. Before long I decided to devote myself full time to journal writing and retire as an interior designer. Within a year the Diarists' Workshop had moved into its own home, a studio space where students can work at large tables and have access to all my supplies and writing materials. That first core group still studies with me. I have never advertised, yet students appear via word of mouth.

More than anything, my focus as a teacher has been about finding ways to motivate my students to access their thoughts. My methods and materials evolved during the process of teaching. I looked at everything available on the market. Blank books with writing prompts at the top of each page just didn't do it for me — what if I want to write more than one page per subject? In fact, *none* of the existing formats worked for me, and I began a personal search for the perfect teaching aide.

That's how the cards evolved, what we now call the Diarist's Deck. As a sixth-grade teacher for more than ten years, I had kept a file of pictures and other illustrations clipped from magazines to use as creative writing prompts for my students. Now I began to design cards with single words or phrases on them to help my diarists focus on a single topic to explore during class. I spent a long time meditating on and designing each one, because the cards themselves needed to be as visually stimulating and as inspirational as the topics are.

The keys to successful journal writing are *wanting* to go to your journal and having a tactile experience using words and pictures. That's why the cards are so effective.

So, why wait any longer? Let your adventures begin!

Charlene Geiss
Santa Fe, New Mexico

Inner Outings

Introduction

Keeping a Journal

*Keeping a journal will absolutely change your life
in ways that you've never imagined.* — Oprah Winfrey

*J*ournal writing is an activity that began long, long ago.
Men and women of centuries past used their pens to record
their feelings, relate their lifestyles and conversations, catalog
their ideas and personal philosophies, and transcribe their
dreams and visions, the same as we do today. Back then it was
a preoccupation of the educated few who were both wealthy
enough and inclined to take the time to transfer their observations onto paper. Others were sea captains maintaining
their ship's logs and generals keeping track of the travails of
wartime.

Now, in the twenty-first century, any of us can buy a
blank journal in a book or stationery store, gift shop, drugstore, or supermarket. We can even craft a personal one by
covering a simple spiral notebook with photographs, art-
work, or a collage of favorite mementos. The frayed ends of
green twigs and berry juice used by the ancients have been

replaced by an assortment of inexpensive pencils and pre-inked pens. Diary writing has never been so easy. Or has it? Often, our journals lay blank, gathering dust as an indictment of our inability — or perhaps terror — to render our ruminations into readable prose.

At the Diarists' Workshop we have heard every excuse. Some blame time as the culprit. We often hear, "There aren't enough hours in the day to get everything done, much less keep a journal." Others use lack of writing talent as an excuse. A few are insecure: "I'm a terrible speller" or "I don't have a creative bone in my body." Some who have tried journal writing complain, "Eventually I end up with page after page of whining and complaining."

There are many excuses, so what are the enticements?

The Purpose of Keeping a Diary

A journal is a book that is entirely yours. It not only belongs to you, it *is* you...the best you, the worst you, the petty you, angry you, loving you, silly you, scared you, serious you, grandiose you. We're all complex beings and our diaries serve to record the intricacies of our day-to-day existence.

The diaries we keep become faithful and steadfast companions to our lives. They are affirmations of the value of our time spent in various pursuits with different people during our lifetime. They acknowledge the lessons learned from our greatest successes and most disappointing failures. Indeed, keeping a journal is a way to honor our accomplishments as we review our past and embrace our present. As the saying goes, it's not where you are, but how far you've come that's important.

4

A journal remains with you always. It is a personal history, an ongoing written record of your life — during both happy times and sad — reflecting your never-ending dialog with yourself. It exists as the physical evidence of your inner outings, those explorations into the private corners of your psyche.

Journal writing makes it possible for each of us — male or female, of any age — to keep in touch with our changing concerns, passions, and emotions. It enables us to:

- Revisit unresolved issues in order to find closure and move on
- Make sense out of our experiences and interactions with others
- Organize and clarify conflicting thoughts
- Figure out what it is we really want and need in our lives
- Express gratitude by giving voice to our blessings

In the written expression of our anger at a person or situation we can begin to work through it and heal. By trying to interpret breakthrough dreams we can gain insight into our unconscious. Put simply, the process of writing allows us to understand ourselves, better, and to gain a clearer view of hte world around us.

The diary is being used increasingly for both therapy and healing. Claudia Kalb, in "Focus on Your Health," *Newsweek,* April 26, 1999, reported that journal writing can help release intense past traumas that manifest in physical ways, such as headaches, allergies, high blood pressure, asthma, rheumatoid arthritis, and other ailments. "Confessional writing has been around since the renaissance," Kalb observed, "but a study reported in the *Journal of the American Medical Association* [reveals that] researchers have found direct physiological evidence that writing increased the level of disease-fighting lymphocytes circulating in the bloodstream."

In fact, many psychotherapists now recommend journaling as a powerful adjunct to traditional talk therapy. This kind of writing is more than simple catharsis: it can unravel the confusion in our minds and transform it into coherent personal stories. Writing about an experience can disarm its power over us.

However, it is not enough to simply record events in a journal without exploring their impact on our lives and emotions. In *Personal Journaling* magazine, Winter 1999, psychologists James Pennebaker, University of Texas /Austin, and Joshua M. Smythe, North Dakota State University, cautioned that "it's not just any writing that helps you stay healthy. What you write and how you write it determines success." That is why the Inner Outings method will prove invaluable to all your journal-writing expeditions, whether strictly therapeutic or not.

Allowing our outer personas to spend quality time with our inner selves is not a luxury or self-indulgence. It is a way to make sense out of our chaotic daily experiences. Our diaries provide a special place for us to monitor our temptations and fears. They give us a private soapbox to air our feelings about everything, including our relationships with our friends, loved ones, and ourselves.

The act of diary writing takes you to an imaginary room in the center of your being, a place where you can begin to understand your interior longings and exterior motivations. But how do you find that room? How do you get started?

The Write Way

Because a journal is an ongoing book you are writing for yourself, there are no rules. That's why becoming a diarist is such an exhilarating experience. A poetic style and fluid prose are not requirements, and the diary of your life's journey will never need editing. You have permission to whine, dump, or vent whenever necessary. No one will give you an F for poor spelling, incomplete sentences, or messy handwriting. You get to completely ignore your inner critic. No censorship or judgments are allowed. Students at the Diarists' Workshop hear Charlene use this phrase constantly: "It's all perfect, always."

Remember that what you write will be just right. Every single time.

Some days your entries will be personal and introspective, either humorous or serious self-examinations of your actions and motives. At other times you may use your pages to succinctly record the people you have seen, events witnessed, or places visited.

It isn't important whether or not you fill many pages during one session. It is perfectly okay to jot down your thoughts in a couple of paragraphs or even compose a short list of impressions if that's all you have time for. Roberta, one student at the Diarists' Workshop, kept a tiny book on her night table. Each evening before bed she would jot down the one word that best described her day. Another student, Claire, for many years kept journals that consisted *only* of lists: places she had been, thoughts during her day, questions on her mind, all wedged in between her shopping and to-do lists.

Anything at all is acceptable. What matters is that you write regularly, and that you write from the heart. All you need to get started is something to write in and an instrument to write with, and you're on your way.

The Write Time

Our days are crammed with physical and mental activities as well as interactions with friends, family, and those we stumble upon along the way. To stay sane, however, we must reserve some time to be with ourselves. Use some of these precious moments for making entries into your diary — just before bedtime, for example, or during the commute to work or school, or while the kids are doing their homework.

The word "journal" comes from the French word *jour,* which means "day." However, for practical purposes, it doesn't matter if your entries are daily, every other day, or weekly. The twelfth-century mystic Hildegard of Bingen wrote in her journal only one day a week, on Sunday afternoons, and yet she filled volumes during her lifetime. That's why it is important to commit yourself to taking the time — or, if necessary, *making* the time — to communicate with your innermost self at frequent intervals. It's not as difficult as you may think, when you fall into the habit. What you'll receive in return is a lifetime of satisfaction.

Why Use the Diarist's Deck?

The Diarist's Deck evolved in the workshops as an aid to encourage regular and purposeful diary writing. Charlene designed these cards to guide both beginning and advanced students into deepening layers of self-knowledge. The cards achieve this goal in both a visually stimulating and thought-provoking way. The journal-writing topics promote a variety of writing styles and inspire new arenas for thought. In addition, they support introspection from an altered point of view.

In the following chapters you will learn how to use the Inner Outings technique to achieve maximum success as a diarist. The cards and this book will enable you to focus on your subject and make the most of the time you have allotted for writing in your journal.

And guess what? An empty page need never scare you again.

Chapter One

The Inner Outings Method

My journal is my life's companion. The format changes, the pens change, the contents vary, the cast of characters comes and goes. Yet this tangible object reminds me that my life is being lived on many levels; it reminds me that I need to act, watch, reflect, write, and then act more clearly. — Christina Baldwin

Regardless of whether you're an old hand at diary writing or just starting, Inner Outings is an interactive tool to facilitate your journaling efforts. By using the cards and book, you'll be able to explore your thoughts more cohesively and write with greater intent. The cards are overwhelmingly popular at the Diarists' Workshop classes and have produced remarkable results. Students love working with them and confirm that Inner Outings does indeed provide the key to opening inner doors. Once you become acquainted with the deck and begin to use this method, we can guarantee that you, too, will write with greater clarity and confidence.

Before going further, get out the Diarist's Deck and take a look at it. Each of the thirty-three cards was designed to serve as a visual stimulus for your creativity. Each of the topics was selected to invigorate your mind, stir your soul, and make you eager to write.

Each card has a corresponding chapter in this book, meant to add additional insights before you begin writing. A "Going Further" section accompanies each topic, which means that you'll have a total of 183 possible subjects to delve into every time you sit down with the cards and book.

Inner Outings will help you celebrate who you are as a person. You'll be able to track where you've been and where you are going. Your journal entries — based on your card selections — will enable you to release past experiences that you carry around as emotional wounds. You'll be able to face the future with more self-assurance, based on the self-knowledge gleaned from your writings in the present. That is the healing effect of the cards.

The Purpose of Inner Outings

The card topics have been chosen to help you zero in on your thoughts and concerns. They'll enable you to resolve unsettled issues and guide you into rewarding inner dialogs.

Depending upon the card you choose, your subsequent writing will fall into one of the following categories, which also encourage:

- ◆ Introspection
- ◆ Investigation
- ◆ Purification

The *introspective* cards — such as "I Remember" and "When I Was a Child" — will allow you to write in a thoughtful and contemplative manner. Your journal entries will tend to be more pensive, at times even meditative, philosophical, or speculative.

The *investigative* subjects include "Heart Songs," "The Masks I Wear," and "Celebrating My Strengths." In this category your writings will be more descriptive, even exploratory or questioning. You might call up anecdotes or report on your unique version of past incidents.

The *purifying* topics are meant to cleanse, liberate, and heal. "My Greatest Fear" and "I Forgive," for example, will allow you to purge pent-up emotions by spilling your feelings onto paper. By giving voice to your suppressed fears or problems, you allow them into your consciousness. The effect is enormously therapeutic and can bring closure.

When to Use the Inner Outings Method

Journal writing is a never-ending journey. Use the cards and book any time you want to embark on a writing expedition — except, of course, on the days when you need to dig into a specific personal dilemma or event.

With Inner Outings, your words and thoughts on different issues will vary each time depending upon your mood and outlook on any particular day. It's both a fun and an insightful way to chart your growth, changes of mind, and personal history.

Life is in constant flux. Keeping a journal will provide a timeline of your attitudes and passions around different matters. In this way, Inner Outings is a means to a gratifying end. It will ensure that your journal is a reflection of you at your sharpest and most contemplative.

Chapter Two

Using the Diarist's Deck

The diary is the only form of writing that encourages total freedom of expression. Because of its very private nature, it has remained immune to any formal rules of content, structure, or style. As a result the diary can come closest to reproducing how consciousness evolves. — Tristine Rainer

*I*nner Outings provides intriguing and provocative topics that will both encourage and coax you to sit down and write. The only requirement for using this method is the wish to get to know yourself better via the art of journal writing. Read this chapter thoroughly before you choose a card and begin. By becoming familiar with the best way to use the cards and book you will achieve the greatest results.

Getting Ready

Settle yourself in a cozy spot with your pen — or pencil, crayon, magic marker, whatever — and journal or notebook nearby. The kind of writing instrument you use and the sort of journal — whether it's lined, unlined, bound or spiral, hardcover or paperback — is completely up to you. That's why there are so many choices available on the market. If you prefer typing a Personal Journal document on your computer or using a journaling software program (see page 130), that is also okay. Whatever works for you is the essential element.

Selecting a Card

Pick up the Diarist's Deck and hold the cards in your hands for a few moments. When you're relaxed and ready, shuffle the cards lightly. Place them face down on a table or other flat surface. Spread them out into a fan shape or scramble them around haphazardly. Center your mind on selecting the right card for you at the moment. If something is troubling you or a specific person pops into your head, simply allow the thought to be there. When you are ready, pick a card. Always let your intuition guide your choice.

The chosen card will be the topic of your journaling session. Uncannily, the subject of the card you draw is usually what you need to address at the moment. If you've picked a card that at first seems difficult or irrelevant, it generally means there are issues around the subject you need to look into further.

The cards are tools for both self-examination and self-expression; some topics have either a positive or negative slant. For example, "When I Was a Child" can bring up good stuff or bad: what you write on any given day depends on what's triggered in you at the moment you are writing.

At the Diarists' Workshop there are no mistakes, no second choices: whichever card you turn over must remain your topic. If you select the same card twice in a row, don't throw it back. Know that you *really* need to address that topic and not avoid it. Besides, each time you embark upon the same subject what you say and how you write will be different.

What if you are traveling and don't want to carry both the cards and book with you, or think you'll be embarrassed by having strangers see you with the cards spread out before you? Then leave the cards at home and bring the book along. Choose a topic by turning to the table of contents, closing your eyes, and pointing, or by opening the book to a random page.

Learning About the Card You Have Selected

After selecting your card, go to the table of contents of this book. Look up the card you've chosen — the topics are listed alphabetically. Then turn to the pertinent page and read. Both the quotes and commentary for each card are designed to jumpstart your writing. These short explorations will enable you to focus more directly on the specific card's inquiry. They will offer the necessary impetus for you to spring from.

The purpose of these explanations is not to tell you *what* to write. They are merely to jog your reactions to the many possibilities behind each topic. They provide a starting point; after reading, you'll most likely come up with your own ideas on how to approach the topic. Charlene, in her classes, never shows examples of possible outcomes because, as she says, who cares? The purpose of this type of journaling is to *have no expectations of outcome.*

If you find yourself resisting the card you've chosen, read the topics in "Going Further." One of the ideas there may spur you on. Don't let yourself fret: embrace the topic and write.

Basic Guidelines

As for *what* to write: anything you desire, whatever pops into your head about the topic you've selected. And *how* to write? It's up to you — stream of consciousness, dialog, lists, keywords or key phrases, poem, letter, telegram — however you wish to express yourself. (Writing tips and hints are in the next chapter.) In fact, the style of writing you use will generally vary from topic to topic. The amount of time you have will also influence your day's output. Charlene always stresses that it's not how much you write, but *that* you write. Sometimes, the most breakthrough and "Aha!" entries are only a few sentences long.

Remember also: No one will be reading or judging your writing style. Don't fuss over vocabulary, spelling, or proper punctuation. Simply let the words flow.

What Are You Waiting For?

All right. If you're ready to wake up your Muse, begin now. Prepare the cards, then center yourself and select one. Turn to its topic in this book and read about its significance and possibilities. Open your journal. Grab a pen. Don't pause too long to consider what you want to say: dive in. Be spontaneous, candid, and always, always, be yourself. Write as much — or as little — as you have time for, but don't lose sight of the fact that honest self-discovery is your ultimate goal.

Time and again, as you make use of the Inner Outings method, you'll be delighted by your ability to write your personal history more fluently and passionately than ever before. You'll be astonished by the things you'll find out about yourself — and by what you will continue to realize and enjoy.

Chapter Three

Hints and Writing Tips

Success is a journey, not a destination —
half the fun is getting there. — Gita Bellin

Additional Considerations When Keeping a Journal

Always date your journal entries so you can keep track of your changing inner environment. You'll derive great satisfaction from going back occasionally to check where you've been and also how far you've evolved on certain issues.

Besides harboring your original observations, grievances, and opinions, you'll enjoy including other bits and pieces in your journal. You can copy favorite poems that inspire you, quotes you find motivational, or snippets from overheard conversations that struck you as either amusing or perceptive.

To complement your writings, consider pasting things into your journal: photos; pictures or headlines from magazines and newspapers; flowers, or feathers, or leaves; programs and tickets from events you've attended; postcards; letters; notes jotted down on cocktail napkins or on the backs of envelopes, anything at all. If you're artistic, and even if you aren't, draw pictures and make collages. It's fun to use rubber stamps, too.

Keeping Your Journal Secret

What about the matter of privacy? You may not care. As Cecily says in Oscar Wilde's *The Importance of Being Earnest,* "[My diary] is simply a...girl's record of her own thoughts and impressions, and consequently meant for publication." You may also be enough of an exhibitionist to enjoy writing in an online journal for the whole world to relish.* On the other hand, in order to bare all between the pages you may want to ensure that there won't be repercussions. It's hard to write candidly if you fear that loved ones may sneak a peek when you're not around.

There are several solutions. You can use a diary with a lock and key or keep it in a secret place. You can also carry it with you wherever you go, which isn't always practical. If you're living with those you trust, stress to them that your journal is private. Ask them to promise not to read it, even if they spot it in plain sight. Or, if you're prone to writing scathing diatribes, you might want to use the camouflage techniques explained in the "Going Further" section of "Secrets" (page 92).

And, if someone *does* read something that's upsetting? It will give the two of you a lot to discuss — about trust as well as the subject at hand.

---

* More about online journals in Appendix I (page 125).

Writing Techniques

As for the actual writing, the following is a brief overview of the myriad techniques — besides "straight" writing — you can use. As stressed earlier, your journal is by and for you. Therefore, you may choose to use any of the following over and over, or not at all.

The techniques listed first are for more in-depth writing. After that, you will discover ways to make punchy journal entries when you are short on time. Besides using the Diarist's Deck, you can make up your own topics to accompany these writing techniques for either yourself or a journal writing group.

- ◆ Rapid writing — also called stream of consciousness, this no-form "messy writing" technique encourages you to let your words spill out at the speed of your thoughts, and every bit as haphazardly. You can use dashes or dots or no punctuation whatsoever. Forget about grammar. This writing can jump around and even become disconnected or repetitive, but it doesn't matter. The purpose is to let the words follow your chaotic thoughts and simply flood the page.

- ◆ Inner dialog — a popular method of writing in which you compose a short scene, as in a play, involving unfinished business between you and another person. Using this technique, you write — in the present tense — both what you want to say to the other person as well as what you think he or she would reply. The imaginary conversation can be as long or as short as it needs to be to reach its necessary conclusion. This make-believe exchange can help you flush out your real feelings on a subject and is a powerful way to go deeply into your needs and motivations. Self-dialoging — a written conversation between your inner and outer selves — is another method that will help you transform guilt or anger into self-knowledge.

- Third-person writing — allows you to look at yourself or a situation from a more objective point of view, that of being on the outside looking in. Your writings will take the form of nonjudgmental observations. Viewing yourself in the third person, that is, writing from the "he" or "she" perspective rather than from "I," allows you to distance yourself from whatever issue is at hand so you can gain an unbiased outlook.

- Imagined letter — just that, a personal message written in the present tense to a person about an issue that bothers or concerns you. In it, you write everything you want to say to the person about the matter. However, the purpose is to give vent to or gather your thoughts; you are *not* meant to mail it. Instead, when you're finished, rip it into pieces, burn it, or paste it in your journal. You can also compose a letter from someone else addressed to you; you "become" that person and write the things you think he or she needs to say to you or what you would like that person to say to you.

- Funny/Serious — simply writing on any subject from the point of view of how you usually are *not:* funny or serious.
- Timed writing — setting a stopwatch or kitchen timer, then expounding on the subject at hand for exactly *seven* minutes. When the time elapses, you stop writing. At the Diarists' Workshop, Charlene hit upon the seven-minute writing rule when she realized that five minutes is too short and ten, too long. It's amazing how much you can write about anything in only seven minutes.
- Rage writing — sometimes you feel compelled to get something out of your system, so here is a way to do it safely. Write every swear word you know, if it will make you feel better, or harangue about a person who's bugging you. Get it out: fill a page fast, non-stop. This is also called breathless writing.
- Nondominant hand — is as it sounds, writing your thoughts using the hand you don't normally use. It produces interesting insights because you are using a different part of your brain, and it is a great technique when writing about your child self. It can also produce some hard-to-read writing.
- Poems — any form of poetry works well for journal writing. Think about the subject or person you wish to address, and then feel free to compose a light-hearted limerick, vibrant verse, soulful sonnet, or happy-go-lucky haiku. You can choose whether to rhyme or not.

- Lists — a perfectly valid way to jot down your feelings, opinions, and thoughts. Going beyond shopping, likes-dislikes, or to-do memorandums, you can consider them checklists for your soul urges.

- Parallel writing — list-making to help you arrive at an important decision. Make two side-by-side columns, one for the pros of the situation, the other for the cons, and list everything you can think of in each column. When you're done, your decision will usually be clear. If not, you will have gained important insights into the matter.

- Press release — announcing you and what you're up to in your journal, as if for an article in your local paper. Give the press release a short title that sums up where you are at the moment. Then outline your accomplishments during the past year and your hopes for the next. Fun to do every so often, both as an assessment and as an affirmation of your life.

- Alphabet listing — putting the letters *a* to *z* in a vertical column and then coming up with one suitable word for each letter. This method is great for evaluating how you're feeling about yourself on a given day, but is also effective when tackling almost any subject.

- Frame of mind — working on the theory of less is more. Draw a two-inch by two-inch square onto a page in your journal. Select a topic and write only what you can fit into that small space. What you come up with will amaze you.

- Songs — imagining the tune of a favorite piece of music, write your own song lyrics: how you're feeling about a certain person or topic and airing your beefs or joys. Then sing it out loud and either let the issue go or be grateful.
- Movie ads — having just filmed the movie of your life story to date, you must now assemble the full-page ad that will appear in the newspaper. Include quotes about the movie (you and your life) from fictitious critics, and announce the cast — the real-life actors who portray you and your friends.
- Geometrical writing — drawing, for example, a circle, triangle, trapezoid, or parallelogram onto a page in your journal and then tackling the day's topic by writing inside the shape. Or, don't bother drawing a circle; just write in a circular pattern.
- Telegrams — since the advent of e-mail, people don't often send telegrams, but this is an effective technique for writing in your diary. Because telegraph companies charge by the word, think of this as a fun way to eliminate the fat from your thoughts. Use as few words as possible — no more than twenty five — to describe your day, send an imaginary message to someone, or explain your thoughts on a certain topic.
- Postcard — writing to a specific person in a space the size of a postcard, telling what you think of him or her, how much that person means to you, and so on. If it's all positive, why not copy it onto an actual postcard and mail it to that person?

- The "personals" ad — writing a short ad for the personals column of your local paper (which you won't actually submit), stating who you are and what you desire. Write as if you are being charged for each word: be concise.
- Banners or headlines — similar to telegrams, but shorter, when you use a short and snappy group of words or an abridged sentence to summarize and pinpoint exactly what you currently think or feel about an event, topic, other person, or yourself.
- Key phrases — similar to banners or headlines, but when you write one relevant sentence that describes exactly where you are with a certain person or subject.
- Keywords — coming up with the appropriate word to describe your outlook on a specific issue or the way you view something or someone in particular. You can choose one word or several, but the keywords must be pungent and powerful.

the diarist's deck

A Gift for Me

If you have two loaves of bread, sell one and buy a lily.
— Chinese proverb

Spend some time alone every day. — The Dalai Lama

*B*abatunde Olatunji's oft-quoted words go like this: "Yesterday is history. Tomorrow is a mystery. And today? Today is a gift. That's why we call it The Present." So, let's not waste it. What better time than today, right now, to think about rewarding and honoring the unique and exceptional being that is you? There are so many ways to do it. Some are material and some not — after all, this is a gift for you and it has to be one that you will really enjoy.

Many of the best presents cost no money at all — an hour with the phone turned off to be still and do nothing, a morning of puttering in the garden, or a walk with a good friend.

You could window shop, bike, or swim in a pond. Take a day off to spend with your children, or an evening to gaze at the stars with a loved one. Time spent in doing something that brings simple joy and contentment is often the best gift of all.

Sometimes, however, you may crave a little something tangible, and there's nothing wrong with that. Play hooky for an afternoon of golf; buy a new pair of dress-up shoes. What about something simpler that will bring you great satisfaction, such as an éclair from your favorite bakery, a gardenia, or that new book you've been wanting to read? Would a massage or pedicure or new haircut make you happy? There is always a visit to a museum, or you could take in a movie, or a concert. The list of small, immediate pleasures is endless.

Let yourself know how much you value your own company. Take out your journal and say out loud to yourself, "This is a gift for me." Write what you would like to give yourself and why you want it.

Now, look at your schedule and set aside the time -today or tomorrow — to bring that gift into being. Enjoy!

Going Further

◆ Sir Winston Churchill said, "We make a living by what we get; we make a life by what we give." Look at the areas of your life: relationships — parents, children, siblings, friends, acquaintances, community, school, work. Choose one and write about what you give to this part of your life.

- Make a list of the ten best gifts you've ever received and who gave them to you.
- And now, the ten best gifts you have ever given, and to whom.
- If you are a gift to your family and friends, what is that gift? This kind of gift refers to your character traits, such as compassion or a sense of humor.
- Write about an experience from your childhood: either an unexpected gift or a gift that you wanted but did not get and how you dealt with the disappointment.
- Write about a person who is a gift in your life and paste a photo of him or her in your journal. What is his or her gift — encouragement, compassion, understanding? What is special about the way he or she gives it?

As I Journey Within

I may not have gone where I intended to go, but I think I have ended up where I intended to be. — Douglas Adams

A good traveler has no fixed plans, and is not intent on arriving.
— Lao-tzu

*O*ur journals exist as evidence of our inner lives. They are the guides to our private journeys. What we write during these sessions with ourselves may be bursting with description, or merely concise observations. Length does not matter, so long as our words reflect the state of our hearts.

The reason we journey within is to explore our feelings. The act of writing helps us make sense out of the chaos that exists in our world. Are there issues that must be examined because we think negatively of others or ourselves? Do we need to contemplate a new insight into the way we want to live our lives? Are there decisions to be made? Our interior expeditions may become extensive wanderings into new continents of our being, or they may be simple strolls down familiar paths.

Every journey should begin with an open mind. From there, we can roam where our thoughts lead us. Even if our trip has been plotted beforehand and our itinerary looks more like an agenda, we should never forget that the point of a journey is the *journey*. When we use our journals as highways for private adventures we can go anywhere. If the trail meanders, so much the better.

As you journey within today, where will you travel? Do you have a map, or will you take your chances and see where the road leads? Try to make your journey as unpredictable as possible. Don't worry about where you will end up. It is the *getting there* that counts. Keeping a diary is a voyage of the spirit, so pick up your pen now and see where your words take you. Be a pioneer!

Going Further

- ◆ Take an imaginary journey to a real location. Where would you like to visit, and why do you think it would be a worthwhile experience? What would you see and do? Who would you like to meet? Who would you like to go with?

- ◆ Now answer the following questions: How would you get there? What must you do to finance the trip? When would you like to go? Do you think you can make this trip a reality?

- Good journeys are often not taken alone. The sharing of places, people, offbeat foods, and sleeping arrangements make our travels significant. The same is true in our inner journeys: all our experiences have been influenced by our soul-level contact with those in our lives. Who have your travel companions been during your life's journey thus far — loved ones, teachers, friends, fellow seekers? List those who've made an impact on you both positively and negatively or write about one person who has etched a place in your life.

- Where are you in your spiritual journey? Are you on such a journey? This need not refer to your religious beliefs or nonbeliefs. Use your intuition to write about where you feel your soul resides at this present moment.

- On the outside of a cigar box, make a collage using magazine cutouts and photos of how you think the world sees you. Inside, do a collage that reflects your private self, your desires, your fears. You can also include meaningful symbols and objects.

Celebrating My Strengths

The art of becoming wise is the art of knowing what to overlook.
— William James

Strength does not come from physical capacity. It comes from an indomitable will. — Mahatma Gandhi

*F*orget about those self-perceived weaknesses that hover around you like ghosts. This is a time to celebrate all the things you have going for yourself — physical, mental, spiritual. You are here today to exult in what makes you the person you are, those special ingredients in the sauce that blend together to form your tasty personality.

Where do you begin? Start by thinking of one arena of your life: it can be your job, school, home, even the gym. How do you interact with and contribute to those around you, the people who are colleagues-of-spirit in one form or another?

33

How do you help them? Inspire them? Cheer them on?

Your deeds need not have won major victories. Lending a helping hand, unasked, is often all that's called for: changing a tire, giving directions, showing someone you care by telephoning. Knowing that you have the ability to show up when necessary, to be a quiet presence in the midst of chaos, is a sign of greatness. Having the courage to let others live their own lives is another.

Visualize yourself as a mighty oak, with roots going deep into the earth and branches extending toward the sky. Understand the strength and patience that it takes to be a tree.

Think about today, for instance, or this week. In what ways did your steadiness and presence of mind alleviate a crisis or situation, even a small one? Did you keep your mouth shut even when you were bursting to offer advice? What did you do and how did you do it? How did it make you feel?

Now, write about *one* of your many strengths.

Going Further

- The Big Picture: adhering to the adage "A picture is worth a thousand words," assemble a collage about you and your life, celebrating your strengths.
- Another way to celebrate your strength is to admit a weakness. Write a dialog between you and your Wise Self discussing what you perceive as a weakness. Admitting to something you don't like about yourself is the best way to confront it and deflate its power over you.
- Write a press release about a recent time when your

inner courage helped you say no under pressure. Every time you override the urge to please others and go with your gut feelings, you become stronger and it becomes easier to do the next time.

◆ Consider your physical strengths. What are they? What do you currently do to make your body stronger? How does it make you feel? What more would you like to do? Think about ways to make the time to do it. Now write it all down, and be proud of yourself. Include a photo, too.

Choices

Life is change. Growth is optional. Choose wisely.
— Karen Kaiser Clark

The last of the human freedoms — to choose one's attitude in any given set of circumstances, to choose one's own way.
— Viktor Frankl

*C*hoice is the great adventure of daily existence. Although we cannot choose many things, many choices are ours, and ours alone, to make.

We choose our friends, for example, and whom we love. We choose our pets, our hobbies, our clothes, what to eat for lunch, whether to help our child with homework or to stand up for a friend in trouble. We observe right versus wrong and good versus evil, and make personal choices.

We can opt to live our life and not run away from it. We

can bottle up anger or let it out. We can share our innermost feelings with friends or remain aloof. In a certain situation, we can decide whether to fight or retreat from it. We can choose what time we want to go to bed, whether to watch television or exercise. It's up to us whether to visit a sick friend or send flowers instead. Life is a smorgasbord of choices.

Real choice, though, comes from following the heart and doing what you feel is the right thing to do. Choice also involves informed decision, which means weighing the pros and cons of a situation before deciding on the best course of action.

A lot of choices, however, involve real change. The better you become at choosing, the more refined your life will become. Bear in mind, however, that you must live with what you've chosen.

Think about it: What do you choose for yourself, right now?

Going Further

♦ What about the *lack* of choice in your life? Is there a situation you can't change, at least for now? Write about how you can learn to accept, tolerate, and perhaps even embrace it.

♦ Pick something different to do today. Take your coffee black. Listen to jazz instead of rap. Try a new restaurant for lunch. Write a letter to your congressperson about something that has been bothering you. Tomorrow, do something else that goes against your usual pattern. Learn to make choice an active part of your life. The more you do it, the better you'll become at it. Write down your choices. Keep track.

Crossroads

Never look down to test the ground before taking your next step; only he who keeps his eye fixed on the far horizon will find the right road. — Dag Hammarskjold

When you come to a fork in the road, take it. — Yogi Berra

Crossroads...zigzags...U-turns...dead ends...clover-leafs...T-intersections...back roads...interstates...blue highways. Often, just at the moment you feel that your life is on track, you arrive at some sort of junction and doubt creeps in. You ask yourself, "Should I stay on my planned course or am I here for a reason? Why is this happening now?" Being faced with unanticipated decisions is a scary prospect, but it certainly gets the adrenaline flowing. Sometimes, going off in a new direction is the best pick-me-up there is, especially if you are in a rut. At other times, you might veer off onto a circuitous route that will merely waste your time or get you seriously lost.

Occasionally we speed up to life's crossroads because the restlessness in the air is generated by our own dissatisfaction with our job or spouse or certain choices we've made. We feel we must upset the status quo in order to stretch and grow. These are dangerous times, for we're apt to focus on the here-and-now rather than on taking a deep look at the possible consequences of our actions. Serious self-introspection is what's called for when we are trying to decide which road to take.

Sometimes, however, we find ourselves at a fork that's not of our own making: we're laid off from our job or our spouse tires of us. In these cases we're forced to wander down new, uncharted paths. The solution here is to remain purposeful rather than reactive.

When you find yourself at a crossroads, a decision has to be made: go forward or backward or zigzag into the unknown. You certainly can't stay in the middle of the street. So, where are you now? Are you at a place that is the result of a good or bad choice made at an earlier crossroad, or are you about to take a new route that is potentially frightening or exhilarating? If your life is a journey, in what direction are you going? Writing about where you are now is a good place to start.

Going Further

◆ Make a drawing or map of your personal path, with the crossroads you have encountered thus far. Begin at childhood or adulthood. How many times have you swerved in unexpected directions or even have taken a

U-turn? When did you avert going off-course by following your hunches and making the right decision? This exercise requires only rudimentary artistic skill, and it's fun to use crayons or watercolors. If you don't wish to draw a map of your entire life right now, then diagram this year. .

♦ List the ways you've managed to stay focused even during those times when you were at a crossroads.

♦ Dolly Parton said, "The way I see it, if you want the rainbow, you gotta put up with the rain." Can you think of times when you stuck it out because you believed things would get better? Did they, or did you finally go down another road?

♦ Are you at a crossroads now? Make two vertical columns and list all the pros and cons of the decision to be made. By the end, you'll probably know what to do.

Doorways

Not knowing when the dawn will come, I open every door.
— Emily Dickinson

*If I can't make it through one door, I'll go through another door
— or I'll make a door. Something terrific will come no matter
how dark the present.* — Joan Rivers

*T*he subject of doorways conjures up many possibilities: real doors, metaphysical ones, doors leading inside, those opening out. Before going further, imagine yourself standing before a door. See the whole scene, where the door is located, what it looks like, what's surrounding it. How do you feel as you gaze at this door? Close your eyes and take a few moments. Now, quickly jot down what you pictured.

When you've finished writing, answer these questions about what you just visualized: is this a door you know or one completely unfamiliar to you? Are you on the outside look-ing in, or on the inside looking out? If you are on the outside, is it a door to a simple cabin or to a large mansion? Is it in the city or in the country? What is the door handle or knob like? Is the door huge and imposing or small and nonthreat-ening? Is it a revolving door? Is it locked? Does it lead into the past or open to the future? Is there more than one door?

How do you feel about doorways? Are you aware of too many in your life, or too few? Do you usually keep your doors closed or open? And if most are open, which are still closed? Is the key kept in a nearby plant for easy access, or is it missing? If you knock on a door, are you confident that someone will answer? Do you believe that when one door closes, another opens? Do you feel that you should wander through any open door or that it's best to stay where you are?

For today's writing, choose one of the preceding ques-tions, copy it into your journal, and then run with it. Next time, select another.

Going Further

- What do you think your perception of doorways tells you about yourself?
- Write about closed doors…both the ones you've closed and the ones that have been closed to you. Think about the reasons why, and how you feel about them.
- What can you do to open those doors or have them opened for you?
- Draw a stick figure, signifying you, standing in front

of a door. Pencil in what's behind you, indoors or out-
doors. Now sketch what you *think* is on the other side
of the door, and then what you *want* to be on the other
side. Is the door a symbol for the rooms you have yet
to enter or the ones you are leaving behind?

◆ Do the following meditation: you are alone, standing
in the middle of a circular space containing seven
doors. Each is painted a different color of the rainbow.
Approach the first door and open it slowly. What do
you see? Go to each door and write about what you
observed, in as much detail as you wish.

◆ Now write about the feelings that came up for you as
you opened each of those doors and witnessed what
was beyond them.

◆ You're now stepping through a door to the most fun
or delightful space you can possibly imagine. What
does it look like? What's in it? And whom? Do you
think you can find or make a place similar to this in
real life?

Explore the Possibility

Without leaps of imagination, or dreaming, we lose the excitement of possibilities. Dreaming, after all, is a form of planning.
— Gloria Steinem

It's kind of fun to do the impossible! — Walt Disney

*O*n the outskirts of your everyday life are adventures waiting to be embarked upon. Some may entail an exploration into the devil-may-care aspect of your nature; others merely require a willingness to investigate potential opportunities. Consider, for now, that nothing lies beyond your dreams. Envision yourself taking on something new. Consider becoming the voyager of your own soul.

Imagine that a major studio is doing a blockbuster film and you're the star. It is filming one of the pivotal episodes today, when you are to utter the universal "Yes!" and veer your course into a new direction. You are driving a snazzy high-tech vehicle along a winding road surrounded by a dense pine forest. The car emerges into a clearing and you pull back a lever. The car turns into a wingless plane and takes off into the sky. You turn left at a cluster of puffy clouds and then soar to a higher altitude. A snow-covered mountain looms ahead, but you deftly land the plane on a plateau, get out, and head through a small opening into the mountain. The cave, instead of being dark and sinister, is filled with brilliant-colored lights. A range of expressions flashes across your face...wonder, amazement, joy. You take in the scene and finally yell, "Yes! This is it! I've found what I've been looking for!" The director shouts, "Cut!"

Now the film crew is gone, but you remain inside the cave to explore. You discover that the cave is really an enormous labyrinth, with passages veering off in different directions. You sense that each contains the possibility of a dream coming true and that each is open to you. So many options are available, many you've never considered. You wander down a path that takes you into a beautiful space bustling with activity and filled with cheerful people. They wave to you, happy to see you. You realize that this is what you've been looking for, and that you are here to...

Is there something hovering in the back of your mind, waiting for an invitation to come forward? Or have you been too caught up in trivia to consider something new? Today, what possibility would you like to explore? Go for it! Be visionary, outrageous, or practical, depending upon your current mood. Let the words flow.

Going Further

- Explore the possibility of changing jobs or careers: what would you choose if you could do whatever you wanted? Would it involve going back to school to learn new skills? Would you start your own business? Write about your perfect job.

- Consider taking a class in a subject that intrigues you but you don't know much about. What would you sign up for? Why did you pick this over all others? Would you actually consider doing it? Make a list of the reasons why you should.

- When in your past did you believe that something was impossible, only to find out that it was indeed possible? Write about your discovery.

- Would you like to take up a new hobby? What would it be? Do you think your friends will be surprised when they learn about it? Write about what you'd like to do and why. Do you think you'll actually do it?

Friends

Many people will walk in and out of your life, but only true friends will leave footprints in your heart. — Eleanor Roosevelt

A friend is a person with whom I may be sincere. Before him, I may think aloud. — Ralph Waldo Emerson

*F*riends are the people who glue our lives together. They are there for us in times of celebration, despair, and everything in between. We run through a range of emotions with them as well — laughter, tears, envy, and annoyance, to name a few.

There are so many kinds of friends: old friends from school or the neighborhood, newer friends from work or community and volunteer activities, special-interest friends — like those who play softball with you every weekend — older friends who have been teachers or mentors to you, friends of friends with whom you've become close, friends you commute to work or school with every day. A sibling or other relative can be a dear friend as well.

People come into our lives from so many directions. What is the alchemy that transforms some into friends while others remain acquaintances or even become adversaries? Some say chemistry — the subtle pheromones we produce that draw us to one another — is what's behind friendship. Others suggest that our attractions are karmic spillovers from previous lifetimes. Still others believe it's simply the sharing of common interests that bonds us to one another. Friends can also be the people we spend the most time with, wherever that happens to be.

We share our lives with our friends. The terrain may veer up-hill and down-hill, but at the end of the day they are still part of us. Write about a person you feel honored to call "friend." Where did you meet? How did you become friends? Are you best friends, close friends, or just friends? Do you think the friendship will last forever?

Going Further

- Write a haiku poem about one of your closest friends. The standard form is a total of three lines and seventeen syllables, usually — but not always — five syllables, seven, five. It's fun and allows you to zero in on the most pertinent (to you) aspects of your friendship with this person.

- Write about a time when you have *not* been the friend you intended to be to someone else. Could it be that you and the other person were never really friends? Think about why.

- List the qualities you look for in making a new friend and the traits you would avoid.
- Phone an old friend you think about but haven't seen in a long time. Now record the conversation and your feelings in your journal.
- What kind of friend are you? Are you always there for the people you care about or only in their times of need? When are you *not* there for your friends?
- Are you currently disenchanted with a friend? Why? Do you think the friendship is endangered? Writing about it will definitely help.

Given the Chance to Change

*We must learn to view change as a natural phenomenon —
to anticipate it and to plan for it. The future is ours to channel
in the direction we want to go . . . we must continually ask
ourselves, "What will happen if . . . ?" or better still,
"How can we make it happen?"* — Lisa Taylor

Only I can change my life. No one can do it for me.
— Carol Burnett

*C*ircumstances force change on us all. A new job can carry
us to another city where we must sculpt out a new life. A
child's illness necessitates reorganization in the structure of
our days. Divorce causes us to reevaluate our attitude toward
relationships and to rethink our current needs. Change
occurs, whether we yearn for it or not. However, even if life
will not stand still we don't have to cower on the sidelines as
meek observers.

Change can be positive: we can regard it as *refinement*. Becoming the best we can be is transformation at its most powerful. Passive change — those situations that are forced upon us — demands strength as well. Any predicament should be assessed with the understanding that we have the power to choose *how* we will react. We can initiate change in our lives by being willing participants in our choices. When we take thoughtful steps toward change — out of our specific needs and goals — we become brave. But, of course, choice involves commitment.

Given the chance to change, what would you do? Where would you begin? Start a list now. What changes — in yourself, in your living or working conditions, in your relationships — do you desire? Leave space to add to the list, for it's as sure to grow as you are.

Going Further

- What in your life doesn't need changing? Are you content with the status quo? Take into account the old saying "If it ain't broke, don't fix it." List what you want to keep. After you make your list, reflect a moment and feel grateful.

- James Baldwin said, "Not everything that is faced can be changed, but nothing can be changed until it is faced." Is there an issue or a person you need to confront right now? How do you think you can change the situation? Write a dialog between you and the person or obstacle you believe is in the way, and attempt to obtain closure.

- Write about a time when circumstances forced you to make an unwanted change in your life. How did you cope? Did the change turn out better than you expected? Does it affect your life now?
- What change did you manifest in the past that's had a profound impact on the way you are today? Write an imagined letter from your Higher Self to you, praising and celebrating your determination.
- Is there a physical change you'd like to make? Write about it — both what you want and how you plan to accomplish your goal.
- Is there any part of your life that's in a rut? Write about it. Then break out, change the channel, and record how you did it.

Heart Songs

All times are beautiful for those who maintain joy within them.... — Rosalia Castro

Occasionally in life there are those moments of unutterable fulfillment that cannot be completely explained by those symbols called words. Their meanings can only be articulated by the inaudible language of the heart. — Martin Luther King, Jr.

*A*n attractive stranger gazes at us and smiles. A friend arrives at our door with a jar of homemade preserves. We snatch a glistening leaf from the grass after a summer rain, amazed by the intensity of its greenness. The spirited music of a neighbor's violin wafts through the open windows into our apartment. A child tickles our face and laughs. Our favorite film is rerun on television. At the seashore, gentle waves cool our bare feet while the salty breeze stirs our soul.

Every day something fine happens. It may be an extraordinary event — *some*body has to win the lottery — or a simple one, such as snuggling up with your sweetie on a snowy day. Regardless of their intensity, these experiences exist to be seized and cherished. The trick is to keep our eyes open and our senses alert. We mustn't get so caught up in our own dramas that we fail to notice the daily gifts appearing before us.

Our hearts respond to joy with many notes and chords. The orchestra of our souls plays its melody. Think about today, or yesterday. What song was your heart singing? What simple pleasures filled you with joy?

Going Further

- When does my heart not sing? What — or whom — puts me out, upsets, or annoys me? How can I avoid these things or people in the future? At the very least, what can I do to keep them from pushing my buttons?
- Look at the past year. What were the highlights? Write about the people or events that brought you pleasure.
- What did you do today to bring delight into someone's life? Yesterday? Last year? Make a list, then answer this question: How did it make you feel?
- Why not make someone else's heart soar send a card just for the heck of it. Prepare your kid's favorite dessert. Phone a relative you haven't seen recently. Do something now, then write about it.

How I See Myself

> *If I am what I have,*
> *And I lose what I have,*
> *Who am I then?*
> — Eric Fromm

> *Nobody can be exactly like me. Sometimes even I have*
> *trouble doing it.* — Tallulah Bankhead

You pick up your favorite magazine, scan the table of contents, and discover to your amazement that there is a piece about you. You quickly turn to the article and there you are: a five-page interview sharing your favorite books and pet peeves and insights on life in general. Several photographs feature you in various situations: jogging along an isolated beach...elegantly dressed at the opening of a new gallery... at home lounging on the sofa with the dog at your side. You are in the kitchen with friends. At work you are giving a presentation as your colleagues nod in approval. You close the magazine. Is there a smile or a frown on your face? Are you happy with the person you show to the world?

Consider also your significant other, family, and friends. How much do they affect the way you see and feel about yourself, either negatively or positively? Would you simply rather be you, without judgment from yourself and others?

On a physical level, how do you see yourself? Don't be merciless: be fair. Pretend you're doing an evaluation of your best friend because, after all, that's who you are. Then write objectively on one of the following for today's journal entry: How do you view your face and your body? And how do you *feel* about your physical persona? Do you hate the way you look, and why? Do you like the way you look, and why? Do you believe others find you pleasing? What can you do — either to change your appearance or to accept it wholeheartedly — beginning today?

Going Further

+ Make a list of the special characteristics that contribute to your individual self, the qualities that make you the personality you are. With detachment, note any unfavorable aspects you would like to improve, but don't be harsh on yourself.
+ Write about your emotional being. How do you handle the ups and downs of life? In what ways do you deal with the stresses and crises of daily living? In what situations are you at your best or worst? Why?
+ What famous person would you most like to be com-

pared with? Why? What are the qualities you admire in that person? Think about whether you already possess those traits, or at least some of them.

- How do you see yourself on a spiritual, nonphysical level? How do you suppose others view you?

- How do you perceive your inner self? Lie in a hammock or on the grass or on a sofa and close your eyes. Go on an inner journey through your entire body, starting at your feet. What do you see? Any blockages? What are the shapes of your emotional, physical, and mental bodies? Visualize, and then write.

- Paste a current photograph of you in your journal. Now — writing in the *third* person — objectively describe how you see yourself.

I Am Grateful for...

Let us be grateful to people who make us happy; they are the charming gardeners who make our souls blossom.
— Marcel Proust

I still miss those I loved who are no longer with me but I find I am grateful for having loved them. The gratitude has finally conquered the loss. — Rita Mae Brown

*W*e look into the goblet of our lives and see it as either half-empty or half-full. None of us views things identically or from the same perspective, which makes us unique as human beings. Our days are brimming with activities and responsibilities. Our minds are cluttered with thoughts. With so much vying for our attention, we have such difficulty seeing the forest: all those trees get in the way. We're so absorbed — with our accomplishments or failures, our dramas and farces, our relationships or lack of them — that we seldom set aside the time to give thanks for what we *do* have.

That is the purpose of this topic: to allow you to take time to count your blessings, since the more we give thanks the more we realize we have to be thankful for. You may be able to make a list without thinking twice. If not, reflect for a few minutes: go back and review yesterday, from the moment you opened your eyes until you closed them at bedtime. Think about what you did and view the places you visited. Consider your interactions with family, friends, co-workers, grocery clerks, caregivers. Bear in mind your pets, garden, hobbies, even your body as it exercised or propelled you from here to there.

Go ahead. Look back at yesterday and make your list: "I am grateful for…"

Going Further

- There is a flip side: circumstances in your life that you're not at all grateful for. Now is an opportunity to give vent to those negative thoughts. Perhaps you'll realize things are not so bad but, if they are, it's healthy to purge every so often. Make a list: what are you *not* grateful for?

- Can you make peace with those people who make your life difficult? Or figure out an amicable way to keep them from harassing you? Can you bring more understanding to the circumstances? Write about how you would go about it. Give it your best shot.

- Gertrude Stein wrote, "Silent gratitude isn't very

much to anyone." What about someone you've lost track of who deserves your thanks? Write a letter, which you will send if you can locate this person, revealing how special he or she was to you. Or write an unsent letter to someone you wish to give thanks to who is no longer around.

◆ Are there other people who may be unaware of how they impacted your life? A teacher or neighbor, for instance, even a stranger who performed a kindness without being asked? List them and write about what they meant to you.

◆ Write about *how* you usually express your gratitude. If someone is kind, generous, or supportive, how do you respond? Some people have a hard time saying "thank you." Do you? And, when the occasion calls for it, can you say "I'm sorry"?

◆ Pretend you've hired a pilot to write a message in the sky to someone you love. You can use only three to six words. What would you say?

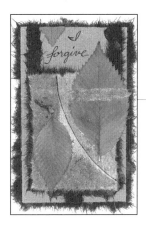

I Forgive...

Forgiveness is all powerful. Forgiveness heals all ills.
— Catherine Ponder

Life is an adventure in forgiveness. — Norman Cousins

Why are we so hard on ourselves? We find it easy to perform self-torture in so many ways. "I should have been nicer to my mother," we cry. Or "I should have paid more attention to what he really wanted, and now he's gone."

It is easy, too, to be critical of others. Our lives are full of everyday judgments directed toward our friends and loved ones. We blame or attack one another constantly — at home, at school, in the workplace — so much so that it becomes second nature. Now it is time to rethink the scenario. Let's use forgiveness as a gateway to understanding.

To love yourself and others is to forgive both you and

everybody else. It's the alternative to beating yourself up in all those clever ways you've invented. Forgiving yourself is a very simple concept, but not at all easy to do. It takes a lot of practice, getting rid of that nagging inner voice that never sleeps and seems bent on making you feel miserable.

Try also to forgive the people who have not behaved nicely toward you. Do it one person at a time. You don't have to pick up the phone and call; this is work you can do on your own, from within. With time, your aura of forgiveness will affect your relationships with those people. It may not *change* all your relationships, but it will ease things for you by clearing the space that exists between you and them.

You don't have to pardon everyone all at once. This is a beginning, but you'll feel better almost immediately. It's all about taking the time to forgive and allowing forgiveness to happen. First you must start with the person you know best. Open your journal and say out loud, "I forgive myself for..." Put your judgments in a box and lock them up while you are writing.

Going Further

- Now say "I forgive (name) for..." and write.
- Would you like to be forgiven by someone you behaved badly toward? Write a letter to him or her that you don't have to send.
- Compose a dialog — in the present tense — between you and someone you would like to be forgiven by or someone you would like to forgive. In this written imaginary conversation, get out all you'd like to say

and what you'd like him or her to say to you. Work toward a conclusion that will help you bring closure to the situation.

- ◆ Write another letter, this time to someone who has hurt you. Tell this person how you feel, how you were upset: get it all out. Visualize the person and forgive him or her, then tear up the letter or burn it. You'll feel much better.

- ◆ Forgive your parents or your children for everything they've said or done to anger you or make you cry. Make a list and forgive it *all!*

- ◆ What can't you forgive? Do you think you'll ever be able to? What — on your part or the other person's — would make forgiveness possible?

I Remember...

*How we remember, what we remember, and why we remember
form the most personal map of our individuality.*
— Christina Baldwin

*The Journal is not essentially a confession, a story about oneself.
It is a Memorial. What does the writer have to remember?
Himself, who he is when he is not writing, when he is living his
daily life, when he is alive and real.* — Maurice Blanchot

Memories exist as the intangible milestones of our lives. Good and bad, these images of our personal nostalgia exist in our heads and hearts. A photograph, the whiff of a long-forgotten scent, the mention of an afternoon when we acted silly — all invoke our reminiscences. A tune will drift us back to where we first danced to it. A taste can sail us to childhood and Grammy cooking gumbo in her kitchen. There is so much to remember: where we have been in our physical and spiritual lives, our dreams and daydreams, even recollections bestowed upon us by our family and friends.

Sometimes uninvited memories flash into our consciousness — good times that are no longer or bad ones we would prefer to leave in the past. Be aware, however, that these impressions have returned for a reason. We must give them freedom to roam. We need to listen to what they tell us. Likewise, we have to allow ourselves to savor happy times that we don't conjure up often enough. Above all, we need to stumble upon the *essence of truth* at the core of our remembrances.

It's important to practice staying mindful of life's experiences. So, fix your gaze upon something that is emotionally meaningful to you. The memory can be of a person, an occasion, a lesson learned, a skill mastered. It needn't be a recollection from the distant past; it can be recent, from today or last week.

How does the memory make you feel? Go deep inside. What emotions does it bring up? What is the truth behind it? Begin writing now: "I remember..."

Going Further

- Is there something you can't forget, a subject that makes you sound like a broken record? What memory haunts you? Buy a helium balloon. With a magic marker, write down what you want to let go of. Now release the balloon and watch it disappear into the ether, along with your angst.
- Choose a period of your life — third grade, for example, or puberty or high school — and then brainstorm

with yourself. Make a list of things you remember from that time.

• Is there something you can't remember or an episode you've stuffed into the back of your mind's closet for convenience? Think hard and try to recall something you haven't thought of for a long time. When the memory appears, write about it dispassionately. If it's painful, observe it; if it's happy, enjoy it like crazy.

• Write about how you would like to be remembered by your family. And by your friends.

• Go through a box or album of old photographs and reexperience an occasion you had completely forgotten. Write about it in detail.

• Put on an album or CD of songs you liked during a specific part of your life. Then record in your journal the images and remembrances that come flooding back.

It Is the Time for Me to…

Why not seize the pleasure at once? How often is happiness destroyed by preparation, foolish preparation? — Jane Austen

We can do whatever we wish to do provided our wish is strong enough…. What do you most want to do? That's what I have to keep asking myself, in the face of difficulties. — Katherine Mansfield

*D*aily living in the twenty-first century is very time consuming. We are here, we are there — either physically or in our minds. We get so caught up in our pursuits that it is difficult to step aside and see where we are or where we're headed. We work, travel, parent, play sports, make love, shop, drive, comfort, advise. We are forever surfing the channels of our lives. At night, we sleep, exhausted … or stay awake anguishing about all those chores waiting in the wings.

"This year is flying by," we complain. We buy a piano but cannot spare one hour a week to take lessons. We cut short our morning jog to meet business clients for breakfast. We whisk the kids from soccer practice to art classes to the orthodontist. We bring our laptops on vacation and spend hours under the palm trees working spreadsheets.

It is time to stop! Hide your cell phone. Step outside and feel the breeze against your face. Be still and reflect. Are you healthy? Fulfilled? Grateful? Do you laugh? Sing? Dance? Exercise? Do you spend enough time with your friends? Do you savor holidays spent with your family? What is it that you need to give your days more meaning?

Right now is the best time to start living your life the way you picture it. With diary in hand, go to a quiet place within yourself. What do you need to change, get rid of, or do more of? Begin by making a list: "It is time for me to...."

Going Further

◆ Think about what it's *not yet* time for you to do: quit your job, go back to school, relocate to another city, tell off your best friend. There are periods during our lifetimes when it's wise to keep the status quo. Make a list of what the timing is not yet right for and — this is important — give reasons why. Recognize that fear may be the reason you are not moving forward in some areas. This is a good thing to know. It will help you understand the nature of proper timing.

◆ Choose something from the list and actually do it. In

your journal jot a note about your experience, but write about it in the third person: "Claudia finally joins the gym and goes for the burn!"

- ◆ To start a business you must create a business plan. So why not write a long-term personal life plan instead? Write about something you want to do within the next year. What is it? How will you organize your time around it? Why is it important to you?
- ◆ Zero in on something you'd like to do — or stop doing — before the week is out. Write one key phrase that clarifies your goal, then elaborate on how you'll go about achieving it.

Just for Fun

If a man insisted always on being serious, and never allowed himself a bit of fun and relaxation, he would go mad or become unstable without knowing it. — Herodotus

Philosophers have argued for centuries about how many angels can dance on the head of a pin, but materialists have always known it depends on whether they are jitterbugging or dancing cheek to cheek. — Tom Robbins

*T*here are times when we are too bogged down with the serious side of life. Our duties and obligations — even those we enjoy — keep us focused and challenged from morning till night. Enough, already! Forget about it! Do you laugh enough? What would make you enjoy yourself more? It's time to get in touch with your whimsical side and maybe even swerve all the way to downright silliness: stretch, giggle,

70

and delight yourself. Step out of your routine and do something that brings you pleasure. Be impulsive!

Spend a morning in bed listening to your favorite music. Gaze up at the clouds. Read a magazine or draw pictures in your journal. Invite a friend over — spur of the moment — for hot chocolate. Take a bubble bath. Make wacky faces into a mirror. Get in your car and drive where you've never been before. Dye your hair a different shade. Host a potluck picnic by the river. Rent five of your favorite comedies and invite friends over for a weekend film festival. Get a joke book and laugh out loud. Put on a costume and dance around the house. Buy a new game to play with your family.

There are so many possibilities. What would you like to do today, just for fun? Make a list of five pleasant activities that make sense for you. Now, get out there and begin to do them! If people accuse you of being capricious, cajole them into coming along with you on your adventures.

Going Further

- Charlie Chaplin said, "A day without laughter is a day wasted." By all means, don't squander this one. Phone a friend who makes you laugh and meet for coffee at your favorite café. Bring along your journals and spend seven minutes writing about a silly moment or funny true story. Then read aloud or exchange writings.

- Fun doesn't only involve laughter; it is anything that tickles your spirit. Think of one or two things you can do today to lighten your footsteps and lessen the predictability of your daily tasks.

- Send a humorous greeting card or postcard to a friend you don't see often. Write a note including some lighthearted news or a joke.
- What can you do to make someone else's day fun? Who will you choose? What will you do?
- Reread a favorite children's book and write about how it makes you feel now. Alternatively, jot down your favorite nursery rhyme.

Letting Go

So letting go is what the whole game is. — John Lennon

Open your arms to change, but don't let go of your values.
— The Dalai Lama

*T*he concept of letting go can be a liberating one. You can let go of your anger at someone and move on. You can let go of unnecessary belongings and simplify your lifestyle. You can let go of your inhibitions and open yourself to new experiences.

The idea of letting go can also be scary. The shedding process can bring exhilarating freedom, but it can also provoke one's anxiety around those sticky issues of possession and control. Letting ourselves go also means releasing our psychological grasp on others, allowing them to be free to do what they need to do without our interference. It's a difficult matter for some of us, less so for others.

Birds lose their feathers, snakes shed their skins, and trees drop their leaves, all as part of nature's yearly cycle. And don't forget: the feathers, skins, and leaves all grow back. Don't we feel our most confident when wearing clothes that are in style for the current season? Then why do we hold onto outmoded beliefs? Why do we cling to relationships that are no longer satisfying us? Why do we cower inside the box instead of breaking out?

Getting rid of attitudes and lifestyles that are no longer working to your advantage is part of the human cycle of growth and change. It's never easy to let go of a friend, a job, or a point of view that has served you well in the past. On the other hand, why hold on to anything that's not fulfilling you now or may even be holding you back?

What circumstances in your life need reexamining as part of your letting-go process?

Going Further

♦ What or whom might you want to let go of to make room for new experiences that will satisfy the person you are now?

♦ Letting go of the old can give you more time for the new. Consider taking on something — volunteer work, a new hobby, getting back to a project you abandoned, even making a new friend. If you could do something new, what would it be?

♦ Are there areas of your life where you *can't* let go — even though you'd like to — because of responsibilities to yourself or another? Do you see any possibility for favorable changes occurring in the situation? It may be as simple as making someone aware of what you need in order to make it work. What do you think you can do?

◆ Here's a great way to let go of negative emotions or thoughts: buy a jar of bubbles and a wand. Think about what you want to release, take a deep breath, and blow your bubbles and troubles into the world. The deep breaths facilitate a physical release. You can also send out positive thoughts via this method.

◆ Take on a project that symbolizes letting go, for example, cleaning out drawers or closets. You might encourage friends to do it, too, and have a swap.

Moving On

The possibilities are numerous once we decide to act and not react.
— Gloria Anzaldua

Don't let yesterday use up too much of today. — Will Rogers

*I*s there a possibility that in a certain area of your life you're stuck? Do you catch yourself repeating the same woes and complaints again and again? Are you constantly whining about your childhood or some other circumstance that hasn't been happy for you? Are you carrying a grudge against anyone who has "done you wrong"? Well, have you considered moving on?

Face it: there are episodes in everyone's life that are unpleasant. We get hurt or abused or misused. It has happened to all of us, on one level or another, but what's the good of wallowing in it? It's certainly not healthy for us physically, spiritually, or psychologically. And for those who have to listen to us sound off, it can be downright boring. (This may even be the reason why journaling was originally invented!)

If your roof leaks, you patch it. If your car runs out of gas, you fill the tank. There is a choice in every situation, even if it isn't obvious at first. Think about it this way: those who have mistreated or cheated you have moved on, so why can't you? (And if they haven't, isn't it time for you to send them packing?) Acknowledge the lesson; take the loss.

Your history cannot be rewritten, but it can be reevaluated. Everything happens for a reason, although it may take a while to see it. Why not accept the past and forgive the players? Are you holding onto anger, sorrow, or regret over a certain relationship? Do you feel resentful and overburdened by responsibilities you took on? Have you been complaining about your job for *way* too long? Do you sigh a lot and moan, "Poor me"?

Which relates most to you right now? Turn it inside out and see it for what it is by writing about it. Then say to yourself out loud, "I'll be moving on now."

Going Further

+ Sometimes we have to stay put, at least for the time being. Is there an arena in your life in which this is not the time to fight the lions? Do you anticipate when you will be able to make a move? How will you do it?
+ In *The Rubáiyát of Omar Khyyám,* Edward FitzGerald wrote, "The Moving Finger writes and, having writ, Moves on." With this in mind, acknowledge your

journal and its value in helping you sort out your life. Can you call up several instances when something in you has changed or has been affected by the words you have written to and for yourself?

- Draw a map of your personal geography: where you've been and where you'd like to go, inventing place names such as Courage Avenue, Burning Bridge, Decision Street, Valley of Faith, Plateau of Experience, Cliffs of Fear, Sea of Possibilities, and Channel of Success. Your map can be geographical, a map of subways or bus stops, or even a treasure map. This is an enlightening way to have fun.

My Greatest Fear

Nothing in life is to be feared. It is only to be understood.
— Marie Curie

You gain strength, courage and confidence by every experience in which you really stop to look fear in the face.... You must do the thing you think you cannot do. — Eleanor Roosevelt

*H*ow often do you recoil from the people or ideas that you fear? Or tuck away your worries in a secret mental envelope, pretending they aren't there? Is it change that's frightening? Is it the uncertainty of the future that raises prickles on the back of your neck and makes your gut uneasy? Are you afraid to fail? Or to succeed? Do certain people make you uncomfortable because of their potential influence over you? Are you scared that you lack control over your life? Do you become unhinged in planes or sailboats, on ladders, or speaking in front of groups? Well, you're not alone.

All of us are frightened occasionally. There are many things to be afraid of in this world: the dangers are both physical and psychological. Still, we have to live our lives the best we can. We can't allow ourselves to become emotionally paralyzed. By facing each inner or outer terror as it appears, we grow stronger: the power of that fear over us begins to shrink.

Those sickening feelings, such as dread and apprehension, can be great motivators. They can provide the concentration and lift needed to propel us over huge hurdles. When we acknowledge panic or anxiety we're no longer hiding them in that dark corner of our soul.

Bring your fears into the light. Air them out like laundry on a windy spring day. Think about the ones you hold within, both real and imaginary. Write down all the icky feelings that come up. After that, decide what's real to you and what is merely the product of an active imagination. Do you need your fears or do you want to be free? Bravery comes from within.

Going Further

- Close your eyes and imagine a life without fear in a specific situation. Now write in detail — in the past tense — about what you saw and did, and how it felt to be fearless in this situation.

- Write about a time when you *were* fearless. Describe the memory: where you were, what you did, how you felt mentally and emotionally. Use lots of adjectives and adverbs. The fearless person you were then is the person you are now.

- Look to others as examples: family, friends, teachers. Is there someone among them you believe to be fearless? What do you admire about him or her? Write about this person.

- Here is a cut-and-paste exercise. This method, called positive patterning, can be used for all sorts of phobias and fears. For example, if you are afraid of swimming, clip a picture out of a magazine of a person swimming and paste it in your journal. Now glue a picture of your face over the swimmer's. Turn to this page often, believe you are that swimmer, and visualize yourself swimming. Now make an appointment to take lessons.

- Write an intimate letter to your specific fear or phobia, explaining in a very personal way exactly how it makes you feel. Wind up by asking for support in overcoming the fear. This exercise can be very healing.

Prayer

Faith is an oasis in the heart which can never be reached by the caravan of thinking. — Kahlil Gibran

Prayer is not asking. It is a longing of the soul. — Mahatma Gandhi

Say a prayer, put a thought into motion, and by definition there will be some effect. Thoughts, wishes, and ideas create worlds.
— Lama Surya Das

Prayer is a bridge to the Absolute, a way of connecting with something higher, wiser, more powerful than the individual self.
— Larry Dossey, M.D.

*P*rayer is a universal theme in all our lives, to varying degrees. It is recognition of and tribute to the Divine as well as to the source that dwells within each of us. Our particular religion or philosophy does not affect the power of the spiritual communication achieved during prayer. It's not important when, why, or even to whom we pray. What's important is that we do it.

What do we pray for? We pray for peace, for health, for the safety of loved ones and friends, for guidance and direction, for many personal reasons. A prayer can be as simple as a grateful "Thank you." It can also manifest as an ongoing dialog with the Divine that lasts a few minutes or hours or our entire lives.

There are those who cynically warn us to pray cautiously because our prayers may be answered. But when we gaze into our hearts and share our feelings with the Divine, our prayers are expressed from a place of authenticity.

Daily we must acknowledge our own source with gratitude and love. In that way we galvanize our energies into the core of our being, that place where prayer takes action. Find a quiet space where you will not be interrupted. Take some time and travel within. Sit with your wishes and needs and appreciation. What would you pray for right now?

Begin writing when you are truly quiet: "My prayer for today is...."

Going Further

- Light a candle in memory of a loved one no longer with you. Visualize that person and think about all the ways he or she was important to you. Remember the love and experiences you shared. Now write about your feelings for this special being.
- What was the first prayer you remember learning as a

child? Record it in your journal, as a flashback. Embellish it to make it look more like an illuminated page.

◆ Make a visual prayer. Find an image of something you need, want, desire, or pray for. Glue the picture in your journal. Create a specific page and look at it often.

◆ We don't pray only for ourselves. Write your personal prayer for someone close to you or someone you've never met, for an endangered species or the planet, or world peace — whatever you want to pray for today.

◆ In your journal write a letter of thanks to whomever you pray to for a prayer that was answered, including the ways that your answered prayer has affected your life.

◆ Was one of your prayers answered in a mysterious or miraculous way? Recall the experience, your surprise, and its influence on your life as it is now.

Puzzled

When nothing is sure, everything is possible.
— Margaret Drabble

*All uncertainty is fruitful...so long as it is accompanied by the
wish to understand.* — Antonio Machado

*T*here are moments in our lives when absolutely nothing
makes sense to us. Why is my boss acting this way we wonder. Why is my spouse mad at me? Why do my friends laugh
when I'm not trying to be funny? It's as if we have entered
the day through an abandoned side door, stepping through
dense cobwebs into a world where our perceptions seem out
of whack. All of a sudden we're forced to evaluate our lives
from a new slant. We observe the behavior and actions of our
loved ones and co-workers and are suddenly dumbfounded.
Or we stare into our own motivations and preoccupations

with total incomprehension. "What's really going on here?" we ask ourselves.

Learn to appreciate these upside-down-inside-out phases when the people and circumstances we sometimes take for granted seem baffling. By allowing our uncertainty — and by assuring ourselves that we are not being absurd — we can begin to explore our confusion and take the steps necessary to emerge from the fog. Only then will we find answers and grow from the experience.

So many things bewilder us; the world is awash in confusion. But puzzles exist to be solved, or at least we must try and solve them. What do you need to look at on this topsy-turvy day? What is puzzling you?

The solution is either inside you or out there somewhere. Be willing to find it and let yourself be puzzled no longer. Close your eyes and think about the first piece toward solving the puzzle. When you're ready, start writing.

Going Further

- Have you recently solved something that has been puzzling you? Take the time now to record it and make it part of your personal history.
- Practice rapid writing and don't stop until you're finished. Write the phrase "I am puzzled by...." Underneath, make a list of fifteen things. Quick! Do it!
- Using the rapid writing technique, make a list of fifteen things you've figured out about yourself and others: "I am no longer puzzled by...."
- When was the last time you did a jigsaw puzzle? Do

one just for fun with a friend, child, or spouse. Afterward, jot down a few notes about the experience.

- Adhering to the adage "One picture is worth a thousand words," assemble a collage in your journal — using photos, and cutouts from magazines and more — depicting the Big Picture, the story of your life either as it is now or how you wish it to be.

Questions

The important thing is to not stop questioning. — Albert Einstein

*Bromidic though it may sound, some questions don't have
answers, which is a terribly difficult lesson to learn.*
— Katherine Graham

*A*sking questions saves lives. That may sound flip but it's
true: coming up with the answers to Why? What? When?
Where? and How? certainly enables us to live better. This
applies to everything from relationships to science and medi-
cine. Our concerns can be about everyday issues or they can
be spiritual inquiries into our purpose in life and where we
are going. Although some questions are unanswerable,
we never stand a chance of finding an answer unless we ask.
Posing relevant questions opens the door to understanding
many things we find confusing. The act of asking indicates

that we're not satisfied with the status quo. By hunting for answers we live our lives on a more committed level.

There are people who are so uninterested in life — or overwhelmed by it — that they never ask questions. Others are afraid of appearing uninformed, ignorant, or uneducated. Still others, for the sake of hearing their own voice, ask but have no regard for the answers. Thoughtful people use their questions as shovels for digging deeper into the ground of truth. Others, however, are content with unearthing only shallow bits of information or gossip — those everyday trivialities that ebb and flow.

What questions do you have? Are they about who you really are? The different facets of your life? Your friends and loved ones? A specific problem that is troubling you? By the very act of posing the question, you open yourself to a possible answer. Some answers come quickly; others take time. Be patient, and remember that there are some answers you'll never know.

Begin a list of questions now, and come back to it regularly. Cross off the ones that have been answered and add new ones as they occur to you. Having curiosity about all aspects of your life can be an ongoing process that is never neglected. Go to it!

Going Further

◆ Make a list of answers: here are some things I *know* — about myself, my friends, family, school, career or job, life, the way I relate to others, the way I see the world. Choose one to write about today.

- Look at the list you made and ask yourself: Do I know more than I am admitting, or are there things I pretend to know, but don't?
- What are the questions in your life that don't have answers? Are you content with not having the answers? Do you think you can come up with the answers?
- Caroline Myss talks about "living with the mystery." How are you at dealing with life's mystery? Can you accept the questions that don't have answers, or do you worry about the unknown?

Secrets

There are no secrets that time does not reveal. — Jean Racine

> *I want to write, but more than that,*
> *I want to bring out all kinds of things*
> *that lie buried in my heart.*
> — Anne Frank

When we were children, we used to dance around the playground singing with glee, "I know a secret...I know a secret!" That information gave us power — both over the one whose secret it was and over those who did not yet know it. There were other times, however, when holding a secret was unbearable because we cared both about the person who shared it and the person who would be hurt by the knowledge of it. But as we grew older, most of us figured out where we stand on the subject of secrets. Some of us relish the juiciness of harboring confidential information, either ours or someone else's. Others prefer not to be burdened with the responsibility of knowing something that must not be revealed. Still others adore both kissing and telling.

Is there something nobody knows about you? The secret can be one you perceive as self-undoing, a soul urge, longed-for changes, or an insight into your self. Or do you have a secret you're having a hard time keeping? Is there one you've kept — yours or another's — for so long that it has become much bigger than it needs to be in your life? Is there something you're keeping from yourself, or perhaps avoiding?

The bottom line is this: Secrets burn a hole in your soul.

Do you have a secret — yours or someone else's — that you need to look at? Journal writing is good therapy for secrets. Unburden yourself. Breathe. Relax. Write. Then read on for tips on camouflaging your writings to keep them a secret from prying eyes.

Going Further

♦ Benjamin Franklin wrote, "Let thy discontents be thy secrets." This is good advice, but every so often you need to blow off steam about a person or thing that is bugging you. The most diplomatic way is to write it. When you're finished, cut up a picture from a magazine and glue the pieces — collage style — over your ranting. You'll feel better, and your discontents *will* indeed remain secrets.

♦ A good friend has told you something hush-hush and it's growing inside of you, bursting to be divulged.

Because honor requires that you not spill the beans, share it with your journal. Write part of it vertically and the remainder horizontally — in crosshatch fashion — so no one will be able to read it.

- Is your secret about flaws in yourself? Write about those flaws, as you perceive them. Afterward, pretend that you are your mother / brother / spouse / best friend reading the list. Would any of them recognize these flaws in you? Are they real or imagined? If real, what can you do to banish them?

- Go to the beach and with a stick write your secret in the sand during the few seconds before the next wave reaches it and washes it away. If you don't live near a beach, buy a small blackboard, write down your secret, and then erase it.

Taking Chances

Accept that all of us can be hurt, that all of us can — and surely will at times — fail. I think we should follow a simple rule: if we can take the worst, take the risk. — Dr. Joyce Brothers

Necessity is the mother of taking chances. — Mark Twain

"Don't do anything rash...think about it for a while." "Go ahead. What are you waiting for? Take a chance!"

Which do you most often hear from your family and friends? Being told one or the other is the telltale sign of whether or not you are a risk taker. Or is it? Some of us are skydivers and some are couch potatoes. Most of us feel that we fall somewhere in between, taking chances when we need to but not for the sheer adrenaline of it.

You don't have to be a Vegas gambler or a rock climber or a police officer to live on the edge. Even if you consider yourself a passive observer you take risks all the time. When you get out of bed in the morning you are stepping from the known into the unknown. Every day you react to and grapple with events that come from the outside world. You drive your car and face the possibility of being broadsided by someone running a red light. You gamble on being hurt when you fall in love or make a new friend. You take a new job that may not work out. You and your spouse decide to start a family. You contemplate becoming a partner in your best friend's new business. You shoot a game of pool and know that you will either win or lose. You invest in the stock market. You have a great idea for an invention and have to decide whether to put your time, energy, and money behind it in order to make it work. You transfer to a different college. You try out a new recipe on guests.

Some chances we take are riskier than others, especially when they affect our loved ones. Some of our decisions are reversible and some aren't. But if you pay attention to your gut feelings, what you do will reflect your needs or desires. The more you take small risks, the easier it becomes to take larger, more life-changing ones. Don't put it off. Make a list of some chances you think you can take today or this week.

Going Further

- Even major risk takers like to have a safety net, that psychological equivalent of comfort food. What's yours?
- Rear Admiral Grace Hopper said, "If it's a good idea, go ahead and do it. It's much easier to apologize than it

is to get permission." Does this speak to you? Can you write about a time when you acted on your hunches, regardless of the opinions of others? Did it work out? If not, what did you learn from the experience?

◆ There's an old song called "Taking a Chance on Love."* If you don't have a significant person in your life, write about the man or woman you'd be willing to take a chance on. If you have now or have had a special other, write about the chances you took in the relationship and whether they paid off.

---

* © 1940, by Vernon Duke, John LaTouche, and Ted Fetter.

Tell the Truth

I don't let my mouth say nothin' my head can't stand.
— Louis Armstrong

If you tell the truth, you don't have to remember anything.
— Mark Twain

How can we be true to our souls if we aren't honest in every situation, all the time? And how hard is that? How often do we tell an outright lie or find ourselves bending the truth to fit a situation? The phone will ring and our spouse will say, "If it's Uncle Ezra, tell him I'm out running errands...I don't have time to talk right now." Or a friend will ask fretfully if we think her husband is having an affair and we answer no even if we saw him with another woman.

Growing up, we are taught not to hurt people's feelings. We gather at an early age that a little white lie is often more convenient than the truth. If we play a prank and admit to it we are punished, so we learn pretty fast not to fess up unless forced into a corner. We also become skilled at tossing the blame onto someone else's shoulders.

After years of this sort of fudging, can we be relied on to avoid lying big time? How do we disentangle ourselves from the web before we commit perjury on the witness stand of Life? This is not about hurting someone else's feelings; it has to do with establishing our inner perfection. If we don't speak our truth, eventually we will suffer the consequences.

Telling the truth is not always easy, but when you lie to others you're lying to yourself. Be honest with people and allow them to be honest back. Articulate what you really want, need, and believe, not what you think others want to hear. Become accountable for yourself: let your life speak. If you lie about anything, break the habit, because that's really what it is — a habit.

Write about an occasion when you didn't tell the truth and it came back to haunt you or about a situation when you told the truth even though it was difficult or painful. Remember to always tell the truth in your journal.

Going Further

◆ Go an entire day without fibbing about anything to anyone, even those telemarketers who persist on calling during dinnertime. Before bed, write every instance when you told the truth rather than giving in to the convenience of not. Pat yourself on the back, and do it again tomorrow.

- Can you believe what your friends and loved ones tell you? Do you think they ever bend the truth to spare your feelings in certain situations? Write about a time when a friend lied to you about something. Are you still friends with that person?

- What about the truth? Do you seek out the truth in every situation? It's hard to find: we are lied to by the media, those in power, even those close to us. Today, write the truths you *know* about yourself. Next time, write the truths you know about others.

- Write about a time you lied to yourself. You don't think you do this? When did you last "adjust" your golf score or order a big gooey dessert while you were on a diet?

The Masks I Wear

We are what we pretend to be, so we must be careful about what we pretend to be. — Kurt Vonnegut

Masks are what they seem to be; not so the faces beneath them.
— Mason Cooley

*I*s your first reaction to this topic "I don't wear any masks...what you see is what you get"? Well, perhaps so, but perhaps not.

Here is an exercise: Travel to the attic of your mind, past the stacks of old memories, chalked-up experiences, stored bits of information, and discarded relationships. Make your way to a dark and dusty corner where you see a trunk. Overhead is a bare bulb. Turn it on, unlatch the hinges, and lift the lid. Inside are a bunch of masks, all beautifully crafted with bits of lace and velvet and gold ribbon. As you examine them more closely you notice that the masks are complete faces, with eyes and noses, and each one is you. There you are — serious, gullible, scared, sad, laughing. The trunk is brimming with masks of you in the different guises you adapt as you go about your daily life.

Now think about all the people with whom you interact — family, friends, classmates, co-workers, teammates, and even passers-by. What masks do you wear with each of them? What is it you need to camouflage? Could it be anger, envy, annoyance, fear, or love?

For instance, we wear the face of carefree nonchalance with the one we have a crush on because we feel too vulnerable to show our true feelings. We take on the façade of robotic overcompetence to hide our nervousness around our intimidating boss. We appear in control with our children, even when our emotional world is falling apart. We try to impress our parents with an aura of confidence and authority. We disguise our feelings when our best pal marries someone we don't like, rather than risk ruining the friendship. Then there is the mask we wear when we have failed at a relationship or other endeavor to seem as if we don't care.

Make a list of the most important people in your life. What masks do you wear with them? Why?

Going Further

- Again, consider those near and dear to you. Does your significant other or best friend ever wear a mask with you? When and why do you think he or she does that?
- Ask each of your good friends to give a one-sentence

description of you. Do you agree? Did everyone come up with something different about you? What does this say about the masks you wear?

- If you were to make a mask of the way you think you appear to the world *most of the time,* what would it look like? Either describe it in writing or draw a picture.
- Think about today and the people you interacted with. Did you wear a mask with any of them? Write about the circumstances.

This Excites Me!

Nothing great was ever achieved without enthusiasm.
— Ralph Waldo Emerson

*I live a day at a time. Each day I look for a kernel of excitement.
In the morning I say: 'What is my exciting thing for today?' Then,
I do the day. Don't ask me about tomorrow.* — Barbara Jordan

*T*here are many levels of excitement. On one end of the
spectrum is the ecstasy of making love; on the other, the high
of competing, and winning. What excites you might not
delight someone else. What revs up another might cool you
down. Of course, our national enthusiasms, such as baseball,
parades, county fairs, Fourth of July picnics, and rallies for
just causes, are enjoyed by many. A lot of us share a passion
with our fellow citizens for ice cream, popcorn, or apple pie.

As individuals we feel sensual excitement for our lovers

and intellectual or physical stimulation from our careers or hobbies. We derive great pleasure from being with our families and friends, even with our pets. Anything that appeals to our five senses can delight us — art, music, literature, poetry, theater, films, architecture, gardens, or food, for example. Some enjoy the simplicity of reading a good book or doing the Sunday crossword; others find their thrills in sports — a tennis player can be just as fervent as someone climbing Mount Everest. Passions that bring about a feeling of well-being — such as sex and chocolate — activate our endorphins, which raise our chi or enhance our mood.

People have various thresholds for excitement. Some may love running slowly down a country road; others need to be training for the Boston Marathon to find satisfaction. One person may be infatuated with collecting classic cars; getting under the hood and repairing the carburetor excites another. Different things excite different people: ballroom dancing, tattoos, finding bargains, collecting antiques, home improvement projects, acting in plays, listening to opera. Some of us have a passion for fashion.

What lights your fire? Start a list now, and come back to it as you add new enthusiasms.

Going Further

- What bores you? Make a list. Now consider removing the word *boring* from your vocabulary and learn to see everything as a possibility for excitement.
- "Approach love and cooking with reckless abandon," encouraged the Dalai Lama. Do you? Is there anything

else you approach with reckless abandon? Or would like to?

- Addictions are passions gone askew. People who go overboard on any subject, from religion to football, have stepped over the line from enthusiasm to obsession. Passion has another dark side, as witnessed by those who get a thrill from living on the edge of physical or psychological danger — gambling, driving too fast, having a preference for guns and violence, of winning at all costs. Is there something that excites you that may not be good for you? Face it, and write.

- Denis Diderot wrote, "Only passions, great passions, can elevate the soul to great things." Do you have any great passions you would like to share with your journal now?

Three Years from Now...

Life is a promise; fulfill it. — Mother Teresa

What lies behind us and what lies before us are small matters compared to what lies within us. — Ralph Waldo Emerson

*T*hree years from now... where will you be? "Who knows?" you answer, "I'm not a psychic." Or *are* you? After all, what you're doing today — or not doing or wanting to do — is planting the seeds for tomorrow. And three years isn't a very long time.

This topic calls for a special way of writing in which you will use an altered point of view. What you will *not* do is sit at your desk, look forward three years, and write in the future tense echoing your expectations and wishes from the present: "Three years from now I will be married...president of the company...an Olympic gold medal winner." Instead, you will go at it from a different direction — you will write from the future as if the events had happened: "I am now happily married...loving my new responsibilities as president of the company...using my success as an Olympic gold medal winner to...."

Think of this exercise more as memoir writing than as journaling. There is a reason for this. If you write about something as *if* it's going to happen there is always an element of doubt about it in your mind, almost like a devil on your shoulder whispering, "Ah, just you wait and see!"

But going at it from the perspective that what you want now has already been achieved changes things on a basic, cellular level in your body. Writing about deeds and dreams as if they have occurred programs your mind to accept them not merely as possibilities but as accomplishments. Your brain processes it as, "This has happened! I did this!"

So, here you are, in the future and feeling confident and content. Before you start writing, visualize yourself and your surroundings. How do you look? Where are you? Now, begin: "It is (date: three years from today) and I..."

Going Further

- Now look at your life three years ago. What's happened since then — with friends, family, love, health, career, school? How has your life changed — for better or for worse? What changes have occurred that you had wanted? Which ones *haven't?*

- Write a newspaper article or press release about you for a paper dated three years from now. If you're short on time, write only the headlines for your story.

- Create something tangible based on what you want to have happened three years from now. For example, do a mock-up cover for a book you will have published, or paste a picture of your head on a picture of someone else who's already doing what you want to do, or take a favorite magazine and glue your photo on the cover.
- Want to try writing about seven years from now?

Trust

Just trust yourself, then you will know how to live.
— Johann Wolfgang von Goethe

You must train your intuition — you must trust the small voice inside you that tells you exactly what to say, what to decide.
— Ingrid Bergman

The topic of trust is a big one for all of us. The very word can conjure up unpleasant memories of times when we were lied to, cheated, or taken advantage of. Living in this world, however, depends upon trust. We must trust ourselves to make the right decisions, and we must have faith that others will act and react honorably and professionally. We have confidence that the pilot of our airplane hasn't knocked back several scotches before going into the cockpit. We trust our teachers to educate our children well and treat them kindly.

We believe that our spouses are not committing adultery. We expect that our banker will not embezzle from our account.

Yet the evidence of misdoings by one person to another surrounds us. The television news is full of it. Most crimes of passion are committed by people who live together, not by strangers. If that is the case, how can you trust your spouse or child or sibling not to get hold of a rifle and blow you away while you're checking your e-mail?

However, if we become paranoid or cynical or hide behind a self-imposed wall, how can we live life to the fullest? How can we be open enough to love others? To love is to trust and, yes, sometimes we are hurt by the deeds of those whom we've trusted. People have probably been burned by our words or actions as well. None of us is perfect, but we try. Trying also means trusting, and forgiving.

Trust lies within us. We are born trusting that we will be fed and sheltered. We develop distrust as we go along; usually it comes when we believed someone blindly or when we went against our own intuition and better judgment. We have to learn to trust our gut instincts and follow our hunches if we are to get the most out of our time on this planet.

Do you trust yourself? Write about how you do, or sometimes don't, follow your instincts.

Going Further

- Have you trusted someone — no longer in your life — who betrayed you? Why do you think he or she did it? Can you forgive (even if only via an unsent letter)?
- How about making a list of the occasions when you've

followed your instincts — possibly against the advice of others or when it was the unpopular thing to do?

- Have you ever done anything rotten to another person? How did it make you feel? Did you eventually confess and apologize?
- Eleanor Roosevelt said, "If someone betrays you once, it is his fault; if he betrays you twice, it is your fault." How do you feel about that? Is there a person in your life who fits this description?

What?

Why, what could she have done, being what she is?
— William Butler Yeats

Where I was born and where and how I have lived is unimportant. It is what I have done with where I have been that should be of interest. — Georgia O'Keeffe

What now? What's up? What if? What's this? What happened? What did you say? What do you want? Whatever.

What plays a big part in our daily lives. We are always questioning ourselves as well as those around us. We ask "What...?" and expect some sort of explanation. We inquire about things that cannot be explained easily, or at all. "What could I have been thinking when I did that?" "What if I had done it differently?" "What should we do now?" "What would happen if...?"

What — as a word and concept — has caused the human

race to evolve. It propels us as individuals to stretch and grow. What events or particular circumstance shaped your life as it is now? What person has influenced you the most? What place has had a profound effect on you?

What would you do if you could go back and change certain episodes of your personal history? What have you learned from your mistakes? What knowledge have you gleaned from your successes? What do you really know about yourself? What can you count on in friends and loved ones?

What do you need to write about right now? Look at the previous possibilities and choose one to write about today. Or come up with your very own "What?" Don't think too hard about it: pounce on this topic! Write freely.

Going Further

- ◆ What is on your mind today? There's probably one major thing, but what about all those minor ones? Make a list and check off what needs your attention. Come back to your list in a week or so and see what can be scratched off as finished business.

- ◆ Create a collage depicting what's on your mind at the moment. Cut up those magazines that have been gathering dust and select words, images, and symbols that reflect your present mindscape.

- ◆ Don't ask yourself any more questions. Instead, spend the next few days being a good listener. Wherever you go, whomever you're with, listen harder to what's around you and what people are saying. Really hear! Write about your new discoveries.

When I Was a Child

Backward, turn backward, O Time, in your flight, Make me a child again just for tonight! — Elizabeth Akers Allen

It's never too late to have a happy childhood. — Tom Robbins

*G*o back to the playground. Swing to and fro with the freedom of carefree nonchalance. Experience the seesaw of enthusiasms and contradictions that fill a child's day. We often reminisce: "When I was a child life seemed so effortless" or "When I was a child I laughed all the time" or "I was never a child; I had too much responsibility." A geyser of feelings is likely to erupt every time we venture back to our early years. Every one of us can evoke childhood memories that are punctuated by glee and sadness, by wonder, amusement, bewilderment, or pain.

Some prefer to adopt the motto "Never look back."

Others cling to the past or use it as an excuse for today's dramas. The little person we once were still exists within us, and there are occasions when we react to life's conundrums from that small child's point of view. This can be good or bad, depending upon the situation. Maintaining a sense of delight in the grownup world keeps our perceptions fresh. Reacting to situations with childish immaturity can inhibit both our inner development and our relationships.

Wave your magic memory wand to travel back to your childhood. Unearth old hurts, then bring them to your present consciousness and heal them. Indulge in past joys; remember how certain lessons were learned. Pinpoint the roots of patterns you revert to today when challenged or praised.

What does your child have to tell you or help you understand? Experience the enchantment, but don't shy away from the sadness. Close your eyes for a few moments before you begin. See yourself at a certain age — a different age each time you do this exercise — and write only in the present tense. Use print for ages up to ten, and script for ages ten to thirteen. Or try writing with your nondominant hand. Now begin, "I am (age)...."

Going Further

♦ Make a batch of your favorite cookies from childhood. Eat a bit of the batter or lick the bowl. While they're baking, write about happy times when you were a child. Alternatively, sniff bags of cinnamon, cloves, and other spices and see what memories they evoke.

- Explore the Other Side of your childhood, the times when you were nasty or needy or wounded. Write about why and how it made you feel. When you're finished, close your eyes and say to that difficult child, "You are loved."
- Get in touch with the magical side of your childhood. Blow bubbles, jump rope, or read a comic book. See a children's movie with a child or rent one of your favorites.
- Find a photo of the little you, either a favorite or one that brings up a negative feeling. Look at your surroundings and the expression on your face. Read your body language. Paste it into your journal and write, in the third person, about what you see.
- Go to the park. Get on a swing or seesaw and indulge in your child-body. Then sit on a bench and write — in the third person — about the child you were.

Why?

You see things; and you say, "Why?" But I dream things that never were; and say,"Why not?" — George Bernard Shaw

My advice to you is not to inquire why or whither, but just enjoy your ice cream while it's on your plate — that's my philosophy.
— Thornton Wilder

Why? needles us. It takes us to that bottomless pit: the unanswerable questions of life. "Why did it have to happen to him?" "Why me? Why now?"

Why? leads us to soul questions, such as "Why was I born? Why am I here?"

Why? allows us to judge others. We say, "Why can't you be more like your brother?" "Why don't you get a decent job?"

Why? opens the door to good ideas. "Why don't we turn the garage into an office?" "Why not take the kids to Europe with me on my business trip?"

Why? can feed our indignation: "Why do I have to clean my room?" "Why is it always up to me to pay the bills?"

Why? enables us to niggle and prod. "Why don't you finish school and get your degree?"

Why? gets us off the hook. "Why bother?" "Why should we go to his party when he didn't come to ours?"

Why? feeds our anger. "Give me one good reason why I should do that!"

Why? also opens the door to hope. "Why can't we try to be friends again?" "Why don't we see more of each other?"

You get the drift. Now it's your turn. Make a list of the Why? questions in your life. Why? Well, why not?

Going Further

- ◆ Why? can also be unproductive. What Why? question do you need to let go of so you can move on? Write it on a piece of paper, not in your journal, and burn it. See your question turning to smoke and ash. Let the breeze blow it into oblivion.

- ◆ Now it's time for a little mind stretching. Research a Why? question that you've been meaning to find the answer to. The answer is out there somewhere; it's up to you to find it. It doesn't have to be a question about your life. It can be anything at all, such as, "Why is the sky blue?" or "Why do they call it mayonnaise?"

- ◆ Do you ask yourself why you don't drive/swim/ride a bike? Then why not do something about it and write about your success?

Wish upon a Star

A wish can manifest itself in purpose. — Washington Irving

Reality is something you rise above. — Liza Minelli

*A*s children we'd wish on the first star that appeared in the evening sky. We hoped for a bicycle for our birthday or that the new boy next door would become our best friend. A pristine new box of crayons, getting an A on the math test, or having a basketball hoop for the backyard were also high on the list. Growing older, we longed for love, a great new job, a car.

As our life grows more complicated, we are often too preoccupied to notice the beacon of the evening. Sometimes we barely glance at the Milky Way. Occasionally we are dazzled by a shooting star or meteor shower, but for many of us the outdoor night becomes something to glimpse between television shows and community meetings and dinners out with family or business colleagues. When was the last time you wished upon a star? Do you remember what you wished for? Did your wish come true? Did you *do* anything to make it come true? After all, we cannot get an A in geometry without memorizing theorems.

Wishing is a form of communication with our soul. It can even be a kind of prayer. It was Shakespeare who said that the wish is father to the thought, so wishes can precipitate life enhancement, even major changes. The very act of formulating a wish — transforming a yearning into a ball of succinct words and uttering it into the universe — puts energy behind it. When that happens your wish has a chance of becoming a reality. And by verbalizing a wish, you give voice to your longings and dreams. Of course, you must be specific with the wording and make sure that what you desire is right for you.

The metaphorical sun is setting. Walk into the gathering dusk of that special place where wishes are born. Make a wish and throw it into the universe. Then write it down, listing the reasons behind your desire. Think of ways you can make that wish come true even without help from beyond. Have fun with this. It can be serious, but it doesn't have to be.

Going Further

- Make a *realistic* wish list of things you hope to manifest within the next six months. Now go outside every night for a week, weather permitting, and wish upon the first star you see. Come back to your list in six months and see if your wishes have come true.

- Can you think of any way — besides wishing — to

make the wishes on your list materialize? Write down what you can do, and then make it happen.

◆ List areas in your life in which wishing won't help, when only discipline and hard work can win out in the end.

◆ What can you do to make someone else's wish become a realization? Write what it would be, and then do it.

◆ Revisit your childhood. Do you remember what you wished for as a child? Which wishes came true?

Additional Resources
for the Diarist

Appendix 1

Sources and Supplies

Part I: Information, Classes, and Journaling Groups on the Internet

Search Engines

Here is an alphabetized list of the current best research sites on the Internet. If you want to see what's out there on your own, go to one of the following and type "Journal Writing" or "Joys of Journaling" in the Search prompt. Besides writing tips, lists of journaling topics, and classes, you can even locate and read the online journals of others.

In addition, many colleges and universities offer courses on journal writing that vary from semester to semester. Go onto one of the Web engines and type in "Journal Writing Courses" for an up-to-date schedule of classes at schools both in your vicinity and online.

If you are feeling lazy, skip this and go to the next section, where we have already ferreted out great sites that are brimming with journaling tips, resources, and information.

About.com.: http://www.about.com
All the Web: http://www.alltheweb.com

Alta Vista: http://www.altavista.com
Ask Jeeves: http://www.askjeeves.com
Google: http://www.google.com
Lycos: http://www.lycos.com
Web Crawler: http://www.webcrawler.com
Yahoo: http://yahoo.com

Websites

A vast amount of resources are available on the Web for journal writers. Remember, however, that there are occasional road closures and detours along the information highway: some sites we list may be here today, gone tomorrow, and possibly back the day after. Be patient. When available, we have listed addresses and telephone numbers.

Association of Personal Historians: http://www.personalhistori ans.org. Dedicated to helping people preserve their histories and life stories. Go to "Coaching Corner" and click "Archives" for articles and writing tips for the aspiring life-story writer.

Can Teach: http://www.track0.com/canteach/elementary/prompts.html. Hundreds of free writing prompts to get you going. Though geared to elementary school students, many are pertinent for adults as well.

Center for Life Stories Preservation: http://www.storypreserva tion.com/home.html. Huge site for genealogy, writing tips, sample memoirs, lists of organizations, and more.

Conversations Within: http://www.journal-writing.com. "Journal Writing and Inner Dialog," is an excellent free online workshop, conducted by Gerry Starnes, who teaches journaling in the Austin, Tex., area.

Creative-Journal.com: http://www.creative-journal.com. Canadian teacher Corinne Pratz's site, with free online Creative-Journal newsletter, dedicated to "Achieving Growth One Word at a Time." Provides journaling encouragement and inspiration via articles, techniques, a visual gallery, and more. Updated weekly.

Creativity Web: http://members.ozemail.com.au/~caveman/Creative. Australian Charles Cave provides creativity resources: quotes, courses, humor, and more. "10 Creativity Kick Starts" offers ideas for keeping a journal.

Education-World: http://www.education-world.com. The curriculum includes the "Journal Writing Every Day" program geared to teachers, with journaling prompts, online training and education, plus articles, such as "Safe Writing."

Heart Writing: http://www.heartwriting.com/class.html. Journaling teacher Lynda Heines offers distance courses via e-mail (prices vary) including "Journal to the Self" and "Building Self-Esteem through Journal Writing." Also, a free online newsletter, *Heart Writing.*

Higher Awareness, Inc.: http://www.higherawareness.com/journal ing.shtml. Online journal-writing courses with "automated personal coaching," plus tools and resources for people who want to reduce anxiety and stress via journal writing. Higher Awareness, Inc., 3532 51st Street, Edmonton, AB, Canada T6L 1C6, 780-462-2167.

Journal Magic: http://www.journalmagic.com. Journaling coach Sue Meyn offers professional coaching, tips on getting started, plus resources, guest writers, and guided journal meditations.

Journal Writing at Suite 101: http://suite101.com/welcome.cfm/3768. Carol Martzinek oversees this site, with resources, monthly articles, exercises, and info for diarists.

Journal Writing Resources: http://people2.clarityconnect.com/web-pages6/tbyrne. Good bibliography of books on journal writing, links to journaling sites, and other resources, including "Intensive Journal" seminars on the method developed by psychologist Ira Progoff — a pupil of Carl Jung and D.T. Suzuki — that uses structured journal writing to "enable the writer to access the deeper layers of his or her consciousness." (Contact http://www.intensivejournal.org or Dialogue House, 80 East 11th Street, #305, New York, NY 10003, 212-673-5880 or 800-221-5844 for additional information on classes using the Progoff method.)

Journal Writing with Virginia Hamilton: http://teacher.scholastic. com/writewit/diary. Ms. Hamilton was a Newbery Medal–winning children's book author. Site offers classes, journaling tips, and writing challenges and a program especially geared to teachers of grades 3–8.

Live Your Dream: http://www.joycechapman.com. Joyce Chapman assists others in their "journey toward self-fulfillment and joy." The author of *Journaling for Joy* provides ideas, techniques, an online journaling circle, and the *Live Your Dream* newsletter.

Natalie Goldberg: http://www.nataliegoldberg.com. Writing guru Goldberg, author of *Writing Down the Bones* and other books on finding the writer within, conducts weeklong workshops in Taos, N. Mex. Check site for dates, or call 800-846-2235.

New Life Stories: http://www.newlifestories.com. Ellen Moore's "Journaling Beneath the Surface" includes a newsletter, writing resources, juicy writing prompts, links, and more.

Oxygen: http://www.oxygen.com. The "Keep a Journal" prompt takes you to Oprah Winfrey's extensive journal site: http://www.oprah.com. But if you click on "The Writer's Tool Kit" under "Self Discovery," you will reap advice on how to craft personal, memory, and poetry journals, and discover a pool of prompts.

Rebeccas Reads: http://rebeccasreads.com/services. Site run by Rebecca Brown, who publishes *RebeccasReads e-Zine* and hosts courses on journal writing conducted via e-mail for beginning to advanced students.

Soul Food Café: http://www.dailywriting.net. Australian Heather Blakey's extensive and interesting site, featuring the Muse Toolbox, guided imagery, creative arts projects, an online journal, and the provocative "Antifreeze for the Soul."

Soulful Living: http://www.soulfulliving.com. Dedicated to personal and spiritual growth. Click on "Soulful Journals" to access the open journal where you may write, anonymously or not. Each month the site explores a new topic, with related articles.

SpiritSite.com: http://spiritsite.com/index.htm. Besides finding a vast listing of self-awareness and spiritual books and retreats, the "Spiritual Writing" prompt provides excerpts from books by many authors, including Julia Cameron, the Dalai Lama, Hugh Prather, Ram Dass, and Marianne Williamson.

The Artist As Traveler: Artist and teacher Gail Rieke offers workshops around the U.S. incorporating travel experiences with journaling and collage. For schedules, e-mail riekestudios@aol.com or write 416 Alta Vista, Santa Fe, NM 87505, 505-988-5229.

The Center for Journal Therapy: http://www.journaltherapy.com. The organization run by Kathleen Adams, author and leader in the field. Courses offered at the center's headquarters outside Denver include "The Write Way to Wellness," "Journal to the Self," and "Clinical Journal Therapy," which includes a home-study series. Contact: Center for Journal Therapy, 12477 West Cedar Drive, #102, Lakewood, CO 80228, 303-986-6460 or 888-421-2298 or e-mail: info@journaltherapy.com.

The Secret Diary: http://www.spies.com/~diane/journals.html. Diane Patterson offers "a little about the history and practice of journaling." Includes writing techniques, bibliography, and an interesting treatise on the legal aspects of one's journal.

Topics du Jour: http://www.colba.net/~micheles/eng/dujoura.htm. A lengthy list of things to write about — free and updated regularly. Michèle Senay's other site: http://www.colba.net/~micheles/sites.htm gives links in French and English.

Tristine Rainer's Center for Autobiographic Studies: http://www.story help.com. The nonprofit educational site of the author of *The New Diary,* CAS offers workshops, retreats, personalized sessions, and resources for the diarist.

Whole Heart: http://www.whole-heart.com/workshops.htm Writer Eldonna Bouton offers a series of four-week online journaling workshops providing "focus, motivation, and support." Courses include "Introduction to Journaling and Reconnecting to the Self" and "Paper Dreams: How to Use Your Journal to Create the Life You Want," also, *The Writefully Yours Newsletter,* a free e-zine for journalers.

Writer's Online Workshops: http://www.writersonlinework shops.com. Offshoot of *Writer's Digest,* offering six- to fourteen-week online courses on life stories, with a focus on the "Personal/Family Memoir."

Writing the Journey™: http://www.writingthejourney.com. Free online journal-writing workshop developed by teacher Charlene Kingston. Besides classes and a monthly newsletter, this site features exercises, resources, tips, reviews, contests, and a bookstore — all for the diarist.

Writing to Heal: http://www.writingtoheal.com. Margie Davis's site "Writing to Heal, Writing to Grow" offers therapeutic personal essay courses via e-mail to examine and understand life's events. Among those offered: "Memoirs for Seniors" and "Writing about Cancer."

Online Journal and Websites

The following sites allow you to read or write diaries online:

Atomic Online Diaries Ring: http://www.atomic-webrings.com
Dear Diary: http://www.deardiary.net
Diaries and Journals on the Internet:
    http://worldimage.com/diaries/index.html
Diarist Net Registry: http://www.diarist.net
DiaryLand Online Diary: http://www.diaryland.com
Diary X: http://www.diaryx.com
Live Journal.com: http://www.livejournal.com
My Dear Diary: http://www.mydeardiary.com
Open Diary: http://www.opendiary.com
Open Pages: http://www.hedgehog.net/op
Oprah's Online Journal: http://www.oprah.com
Scribe Tribe: http://groups.yahoo.com/group/ScribeTribe

Part II: Supplies for the Diarist

Blank Journals, Pens, and Accessories

You'll most likely find a variety of journals and pens at your local book, stationery, or art store. You may also locate something that suits you at an office supply, drugstore, or supermarket. However, these sites are worth checking out if you're looking for something special.

Bittner Fine Stationery: http://www.bittner.com. The online catalog of a California store offering stylish journals, pens, and accessories. Expensive, but a nice gift for yourself or others. Telephone orders: 1-888-BITTNER or, in California, 831-626-8828.

Flax Art & Design: http://www.flaxart.com. This site features links to the collage and the paper catalog. All offer many journals — including ones with keys for secrecy — and all kinds of writing and collage supplies. Free catalogs on request.

Journal Depot: http://www.journaldepot.com. An online journal writing store, featuring a variety of diaries and special interest journals in a huge number of categories — including children, dreams, holidays, autobiography, parenting, sports.

Journals Unlimited, Inc.: http://www.journalsunlimited.com. The "Write It Down" series offers a selection of oversized spiral-bound blank and special interest journals. Telephone orders: 1-800-897-8528 or, in Michigan, 989-686-3377.

Kate's Paperie: http://www.katespaperie.com. This New York store and online catalog carries a large supply of elegant journals, pens, and collage materials.

K. Schweizer: http://www.kschweizer.com. An array of quality leather and nonleather journals plus accessories including pens, albums, scrapbooks, and software. Telephone: 888-444-0055.

Levenger: http://www.levenger.com. Top-of-the-line journals and accessories, including a "Chapters Journal" with a unique binding that allows pages to lie flat rather than rolling near the spine. Go online to shop or request a free catalog.

Michael Roger Press: http://www.mrogerpress.com. The company, established in 1949, has a huge inventory of journals in unique and unusual cover designs, including colorful faux-fur, Chinese silk, cork, bark, leather, and glitter.

Old Leather Books: http://www.oldleather.com. Handmade leather journals, bibles, scrapbooks, and custom bookbinding by Sandra S. Kahn, who also runs bookbinding workshops. Order online or contact Old Leather Books, 9 Bradley Road, Belmont, MA 02479, 617-489-1528.

Running Rhino & Company: http://www.runningrhino.com. A variety of attractive, affordable journals, lined or unlined, in various sizes, made "*by* journal users *for* journal users."

Wakimbo: http://www.wakimbo.com. Beautiful, environmentally friendly journals created and handmade in Sydney, Australia. They ship internationally at a reasonable cost. A fun, thoughtful site to visit, featuring a "Journalogy" section with writing prompts, a "Journaling Q&A," and great diarists in history.

Personal Journaling Software

Nothing can replace paper and pen, or can it? Writing a journal on your computer allows you to keep your most intimate thoughts and observations protected from prying eyes (all the following programs offer password protection), which is something to consider.

LifeJournal™: http://www.lifejournal.com. A software program for personal journal writing. $39.95, but can be downloaded for a free trial. Very slick, offering thought-provoking quotes and prompts, a "Life History" module for creating an ongoing timeline, "Dream Journal," and more.

Odaat 95: http://home.nc.rr.com/prd/odaat. A free program to download for daily journal writing that's simple to use and not overcrowded with features you don't need. Supplies inspirational quotes as well.

The Journal: http://www.davidrm.com. A word-processing program for diarists that includes a thesaurus and spelling checker. Entries can be reviewed by date or category. $34.95, but can be downloaded for a free 30-day trial.

VistaWrite: http://www.digitalwriting.com. Allows you to make entries into multiple journals on different topics. You can keep track of special events, dreams, personal insights, birthdays, even to-do lists. $39.95, but can be downloaded for a free 30-day trial. Also offers journal exercises and articles by diarists.

Yeah Write Journaling Software: http://www.wordplace.com. Offers lots of options plus automatic, easy-to-use features. Download a free trial, and then register online for $19 if you're satisfied. Also allows you to download up to twelve dictionaries. Telephone orders: 801-221-7771.

Appendix 2

Recommended Reading

Creativity and Writing

*Berg, Elizabeth. *Escaping into the Open: The Art of Writing True.* New York: HarperCollins, 1999.

Cameron, Julia. *The Artist's Way: A Spiritual Path to Higher Creativity.* New York: G. P. Putnam's Sons, 1992.

———. *The Right to Write.* New York: Jeremy P. Tarcher, 1998.

———. *The Vein of Gold: A Journey to Your Creative Heart.* New York: G. P. Putnam's Sons, 1996.

*Dorff, Francis. *Simply Soul Stirring: Writing as a Meditative Practice.* Mahwah, N.J.: Paulist Press, 1998.

*Goldberg, Natalie. *Thunder and Lightning: Cracking Open the Writer's Craft.* New York: Bantam, 2000.

———. *Wild Mind: Living the Writer's Life.* New York: Bantam Books, 1990.

———. *Writing Down the Bones: Freeing the Writer Within.* Boston: Shambhala, 1986.

Maisel, Eric. *Fearless Creating: A Step-by-Step Guide to Starting and Completing Your Work of Art.* New York: Jeremy P. Tarcher, 1995.

Rico, Gabriele. *Pain and Possibility: Writing the Natural Way: Using Right-Brain Techniques to Release Your Expressive Powers.* Rev. ed. New York: Jeremy P. Tarcher, 2000.

---

* Highly recommended

Diary Anthologies

Bender, Sheila. *The Writer's Journal: 40 Contemporary Writers and Their Journals.* New York: Dell, 1997.

Johnson, Alexandra. *The Hidden Writer: Diaries and the Creative Life.* New York: Doubleday, 1997.

Junker, Howard, ed. *The Writer's Notebook.* New York: HarperCollins, 1995.

*Mallon, Thomas. *A Book of One's Own: People and Their Diaries.* St. Paul, Minn.: Hungry Mind, 1995.

Moffat, Mary Jane, ed. *Diaries of Women.* New York: Vintage Books, 1975.

Journaling

Adams, Kathleen. *Journal to the Self.* New York: Warner Books, 1990.

*Baldwin, Christina. *Life's Companion: Journal Writing as a Spiritual Quest.* New York: Bantam Books, 1990.

———. *One to One: Self-Understanding Through Journal Writing.* New York: M. Evans, 1977.

Bender, Sheila. *Keeping a Journal You Love.* Cincinnati, Ohio: Walking Stick Press, 2001.

———. *A Year in the Life: Journaling for Self-Discovery.* Cincinnati, Ohio: Walking Stick Press, 2000.

Capacchione, Lucia. *The Creative Journal: The Art of Finding Yourself.* 2nd ed. Franklin Lakes, N.J.: New Page Books, 2001.

Guarino, Lois. *Writing Your Authentic Self:* The Omega Institute Mind, Body, Spirit Series. New York: Dell, 1999.

Holzer, Burghild Nina. *A Walk Between Heaven and Earth.* New York: Bell Tower, 1994.

Jacobs, Rita D. *The Way In: Journal Writing for Self-Discovery.* New York: Stewart, Tabori & Chang, 2001.

*Johnson, Alexandra. *Leaving a Trace: The Art of Transforming a Life into Stories.* Boston: Little, Brown, and Company, 2001.

Klug, Ronald. *How to Keep a Spiritual Journal.* Minneapolis, Minn.: Augsburg, 1993.

---

* Highly recommended

Neimark, Neil F. M.D., *The Handbook of Journaling: Tools for the Healing of Mind, Body & Spirit.* 2nd ed. Irvine, Calif: R.E.P. Technologies, 2000.

Progoff, Ira. *At a Journal Workshop.* New York: G.P. Putnam's Sons, 1978.
———. *Life-Study: Experiencing Creative Lives by the Intensive Journal Method.* New York: Dialogue House, 1983.

*Rainer, Tristine. *The New Diary.* New York: G.P. Putnams Sons, 1978.

Rico, Gabrielle. *Writing Your Way Through Personal Crisis.* New York: Jeremy P. Tarcher, 1991.

*Schiwy, Marlene. *A Voice of Her Own: Women and the Journal-Writing Journey.* New York: Simon and Schuster, 1996.

Journal Making

Fox, Gabrielle. *The Essential Guide to Making Handmade Books.* Salt Lake City, Utah: North Light Books, 2000.

Hinchman, Hanna. *A Life in Hand: Creating the Illuminated Journal.* Layton, Utah: Gibbs Smith, 1999.

Thompson, Jason. *Making Journals by Hand: 20 Creative Projects for Keeping Your Thoughts.* Gloucester, Mass.: Rockport Books, 2000.

Tourtillott, Suzanne J.E. *Making and Keeping Creative Journals.* Asheville, N.C.: Lark Books, 2001.

Periodicals

Several journaling newsletters are on the Internet (see Appendix I, page 123). The following is the only print publication for diarists, as of this writing:

Personal Journaling Magazine: http://www.journalingmagazine.com Published bi-monthly by Writer's Digest, Inc., this publication serves as "a companion for your journal writing." The Internet site gives information on current and back issues.

---

* Highly recommended

Acknowledgments

*W*e are most grateful to the following people for their valuable assistance in bringing *Inner Outings* into being: Mary Ann Casler, Dean and Jeanine D'Agostino, Mary Donald, Bruce Geiss, Linnea Geiss, Nora Geiss, Howard Hersh, Georgia Hughes, Norman Kurz, Barbara Lowenstein, Munro Magruder, Susan Munroe, Jonathan Richards, Virginia Simpson-Magruder, Jim Smith, and the dedicated students of the Diarists' Workshop who, from the beginning, have inspired and supported this project. Write on!